"An exceptionally thoughtful approach to ensure that students thrive! Robbins provides a practical and evidence-based approach that allows educators to create the conditions necessary for Black students to achieve success. Our students deserve nothing less than educators who believe in them, address microaggressions and bias, and protect them from harm. In doing so, we meet the needs of our Black students and foster their greatness."

Douglas Fisher, *Professor, San Diego State University*

"I entered education in 1988 as a 5th grade teacher in Brooklyn, NYC, and since that day, my underlying challenge as a teacher and a principal has been the challenge of closing the racial gap in achievement with Black children being perennially on the wrong side of this gap. Many have made the effort offering earnest solutions over the years toward closing the racial gap in achievement but here we are in 2024 and the gap I was introduced to in 1988 continues to persist. To that end, I find Dr. Robbins book to be rather fascinating where instead of focusing on the teaching and learning aspect of what Black children require in the classroom, he's approaching the achievement gap from the perspective of the sort of teachers that Black students need. This translates into the difficult, uncomfortable, courageous conversations that not everyone wants to have, but Dr. Robbins meets it head on with sound strategy, advice and guidance. For that reason, I recommend this book with zero hesitation."

Principal Baruti Kafele, *Education Consultant,*
Author, Retired Principal

"In *The Teachers Black Students Need*, Dr. Zachary Scott Robbins masterfully addresses the urgent need for educators who truly understand and support the unique experiences of Black students. This book is not just a guide – it's a call to action for teachers to reflect deeply on their practices, challenge systemic biases, and commit to fostering environments where Black students can thrive both academically and personally.

"Dr. Robbins's insights, drawn from his lived experience as an educator and parent, resonate powerfully with the concept of 'Racial Battle Fatigue,' a term I coined to describe the cumulative emotional, psychological, and physical toll of racial microaggressions on individuals from racially minoritized groups. By acknowledging the harsh realities that Black students face, Dr. Robbins offers educators practical strategies to affirm their students' identities, build meaningful relationships, and advocate for equity in the classroom.

"This book is essential reading for any educator dedicated to dismantling the barriers that Black students encounter in our schools. Dr. Robbins provides not only a critique of current educational practices but also a blueprint for creating a more just and inclusive educational system. I commend this work to all who are committed to making a lasting impact on the lives of Black students."

Dr. William A. Smith, *Chief Executive Administrator at the Huntsman Mental Health Institute; Department of Psychiatry and the Department of Education, Culture, & Society at the University of Utah; Pioneer of the Racial Battle Fatigue Framework*

"I was intrigued, captivated, and drawn to this book that will help fellow educators expand, inform, and improve their practice in today's complex educational setting. Throughout *The Teachers Black Students Need*, Dr. Robbins stresses the importance of educators advocating for Black students in the face of restrictive laws and policies that limit discussions on race and history. He boldly calls on educators to recognize and respond to racial trauma and discusses the need for culturally affirming relationships between teachers and Black students. As a life-long educator, I appreciated the reminder of how delicate these relationships can be.

"This book emphasizes the need for an educational approach that is supportive, inclusive, and responsive to the unique challenges faced by Black students, and I thoroughly enjoyed the journey Dr. Robbins so eloquently took me on."

John Anzalone, *Ed.D.*

"If you want to receive a deeply personal message from a parent and educator, read this book. Dr. Robbins provides 'windows' and 'mirrors' from his lived experience as an African-American parent and educator. Perspective is powerful."

Dr. Peter Dallas Finch, *Superintendent,*
West Valley School District #208, Washington

"It is with great honor that I write this statement of endorsement for *The Teachers Black Students Need*, by Dr. Zachary Scott Robbins! The contents herein are thoughtful, common sense and certainly possess great awareness of best teaching practices and pedagogy as it relates to student learning. Juxtaposed with real-life experiences and vignettes that are relatable to circumstances we encounter each day with, not only Black Students, but students of ALL ethnicities and life experiences, the stories Dr. Robbins conveys would help a blue-chip experienced educator or a novice teacher learn and evolve to gain empathy so that they can best relate to ALL children. Detailiing common sense practices, readers will enjoy immediate takeaways they could invoke within districts, schools and/or classrooms that not only are beneficial to Black students, but ALL students. The focus is just right considering the decades old systemic achievement gaps and proficiency levels of American African American youth. A must read for ALL educators!"

Dr. Jeffrey Geihs, *Executive Director,*
Nevada Association of School Administrators & CEO,
Silver State Education Foundation

"In *The Teachers Black Students Need*, Dr. Robbins equips educators with powerful tools to transform passive support into active advocacy for Black students. While many may consider themselves champions of racial equality, this book serves as a critical mirror, challenging readers to reflect on whether their intentions are truly manifesting in impactful actions."

Peter Gorman, *Cofounder, The Forum for*
Educational Leadership, and former superintendent,
Charlotte Mecklenburg Schools

The Teachers Black Students Need

Who are the teachers Black students need? In this thought-provoking book, award-winning superintendent Zachary Scott Robbins considers this question and the impact its answer has for Black children everywhere. Robbins articulates the heartfelt concerns of an educator and father raising children in public school, some unsafe, some mired in racial unrest, and some defined by inequality. He shares what teachers can do to mitigate the imbalance of resources and educational opportunities available to Black students and to establish relationships with Black students that are foundational for sustainable, positive academic outcomes.

Throughout the book, Robbins gives readers a roadmap to provide Black students with high-quality education. Topics include helping Black students see schooling as useful and relevant; affirming their strengths and interests; believing in students and celebrating their growth; helping Black students who experience racial discrimination, violence, and microaggressions in schools; using diverse learning materials to mitigate biases; avoiding academic grading bias and behavioral grading bias; making your classroom an academically and psychologically safe space; and using your voice to advocate for Black students.

Through a combination of stories and practical solutions, Robbins helps us re-imagine possibilities – and take action – on what schools can be for the Black students we serve.

Zachary Scott Robbins has "turned around" schools in Boston, Las Vegas, and Washington and was honored to be the 2022 Nevada High School Principal of the Year. Dr. Robbins was the 2021 City of Las Vegas African-American Trailblazer in Education Award Recipient, and in 2021, he was the President-Elect of the Secondary School Principals Association of Nevada. Dr. Robbins was educated at Howard University in Washington, DC, and he earned his PhD in Education Administration at the Boston College Lynch School of Education. You can find Dr. Robbins on Twitter/X at DrZacRobbins.

Also Available from Routledge
Eye On Education
www.routledge.com/k-12

Restorative Justice Tribunal:
And Ways to Derail Jim Crow Discipline in Schools
Zachary Scott Robbins

Identity Affirming Classrooms:
Spaces that Center Humanity
Erica Buchanan-Rivera

Let's Get Real:
Exploring Race, Class, and Gender Identities in the Classroom
Martha Caldwell and Oman Frame

Tangible Equity:
A Guide for Leveraging Student Identity, Culture, and
Power to Unlock Excellence In and Beyond the Classroom
Colin Seale

Teaching Practices from America's Best Urban Schools:
A Guide for School and Classroom Leaders
By Joseph F. Johnson, Jr., Cynthia L. Uline,
Lynne G. Perez

The Teachers Black Students Need

A Guide to Help Students Thrive in School

Zachary Scott Robbins

NEW YORK AND LONDON

Designed cover image: Getty Images

First published 2025
by Routledge
605 Third Avenue, New York, NY 10158

and by Routledge
4 Park Square, Milton Park, Abingdon, Oxon, OX14 4RN

Routledge is an imprint of the Taylor & Francis Group, an informa business

© 2025 Zachary Scott Robbins

The right of Zachary Scott Robbins to be identified as author of this work has been asserted in accordance with sections 77 and 78 of the Copyright, Designs and Patents Act 1988.

All rights reserved. No part of this book may be reprinted or reproduced or utilised in any form or by any electronic, mechanical, or other means, now known or hereafter invented, including photocopying and recording, or in any information storage or retrieval system, without permission in writing from the publishers.

Trademark notice: Product or corporate names may be trademarks or registered trademarks, and are used only for identification and explanation without intent to infringe.

ISBN: 978-1-032-86838-7 (hbk)
ISBN: 978-1-032-85755-8 (pbk)
ISBN: 978-1-003-52950-7 (ebk)

DOI: 10.4324/9781003529507

Typeset in Palatino
by Apex CoVantage, LLC

Some names and identifying details have been changed to protect the privacy of individuals.

Contents

Preface: Words for My Beautiful Children   xiv

**1   Black Students Need Teachers Who Understand
     That Education and Schooling Are Not the Same**   **1**
Help Black Students See Schooling As Useful   2
Ensure Schooling Embraces Black Students   4
Affirm Your Black Students' Efforts and Interests   6

**2   Black Students Succeed When Teachers Believe
     in Them**   **10**
Set High Expectations and Black Students Will
      Strive to Meet Them   12
Celebrate Black Students' Academic Growth So
      Students Can See Their Improvement   13
Be Mindful of When to Push and Pull Your Black
      Students Toward Academic Growth   15
See Your Students' Strengths and Potential So
      They Can See Them, Too   20
Make Learning Relevant to Keep Black Students
      Engaged   21

**3   Don't Let Microaggressions Define Black
     Students' Classroom Experiences**   **25**
What Are Microaggressions?   26
Help Prevent Microaggressions in the Classroom
      by Being Aware of Your Unconscious Biases   27
Use Your Classroom Management Toolbox to
      Prevent Microaggressions   30
Ways Black Students Experience
      Microaggressions in Schools   34

xii ◆ Contents

Microaggressions Affect Black Students Negatively   35
Common Microaggressions in the Classroom and
    How to Prevent Them   37
Address Microaggressions in Your Classroom   40
Diverse Learning Materials Can Mitigate Biases
    that Are the Root of Race-Based Microaggressions   43
Address Race-Based Microaggressive School Policies   45

4   Protect Black Students' Bodies From Harm   51
Schools Are Becoming More Violent   52
Protect Black Students From Dangerous and
    Disruptive Schoolmates   53
Use De-Escalation Techniques to Keep Your
    Classroom Community Orderly and
    Conducive to Learning   56
Know What's in Students' IEPs and 504 Plans to
    Ensure a Safe and Respectful Learning
    Environment   58
Monitor Students' Unstructured Time and Spaces   59

**5   Don't Let Grades Become Weapons Against
Black Students   64**
The Case of Reva and Brook Stevens   65
Be Aware of Academic Grading Bias   66
Be Aware of Behavioral Grading Bias   67
Ensure Grades Reflect What Students Know and
    Can Do   68
Give Students Helpful, High-Quality Feedback   68
Seven Keys to Effective Feedback   70
Make Your Classroom an Academically and
    Psychologically Safe Space   71
How The Teachers Black Students Need
    Assign Grades   72

6   Use Your Voice to Advocate for Black Students   76
Your Voice Is a Powerful Tool   77
Parents, Special Interest Groups, and Politicians
    Are Influencing What Teachers Teach   78

Contents ◆ xiii

Understanding What Rights Parents Do and
    Don't Have in Your Classroom 80
Collaborate with Your Superintendent 82
Encourage Students to Be Informed Voters 85

7 Protect Black Students From Racial Trauma **92**
What Racial Discrimination Looks Like at School
    and How It Impacts Black Students 93
How to Respond to Race-Based Bullying in Your
    Classroom 96
Use Professional Judgment to Discern How to
    Respond to Racially Insensitive Behavior 99
How to Respond When Racial Trauma in the
    Community Affects Your Class 101
How to Respond to Race-Based Discrimination in
    School Hallways 104
How to Respond to Race-Based Discrimination
    From a Colleague 105
How to Support Students Who Tell You They're
    Being Racially Bullied or Discriminated Against 109
"Nobody's Listening!" How to Respond
    to Students' Concerns about Racial
    Discrimination When They Feel Ignored 110

8 Black Students' Relationship With School Police **116**
Students Want to Feel Safe at School 117
The Impact of Police on Black Students 119
How to Work With School Police to Create a
    Better Experience for Your Black Students 121
Teachers Must Know What School Police
    Misconduct Is and How to Address It 128

Epilogue: Final Thoughts About Being a
Teacher Black Students Need **132**

Preface

Words for My Beautiful Children

Zahra, Zaire, and Zamorah, I love you. It is amazing how alike we are. I enjoyed bike rides with my friends when I was your ages, just as you all enjoy Sunday bike rides with your mom. Zahra, you love baking and are masterful at decorating cakes. You "got that honest," so to speak. You watched me bake cakes in my kitchen like I watched your Great-Grandmother Azalee and your Grandma Lucy mill about their kitchens, baking cakes, pies, and biscuits from scratch.

It doesn't surprise me, Zaire, that you love playing video games. I remember playing a video game called Astrosmash on an Intellivision game console with your Grandma Lucy. She practiced while I was at school and beat me mercilessly when I got home.

Zamorah, you love playing with your dolls the way I used to love playing with Star Wars action figures. I love watching you create worlds with your imagination. I look forward to watching your creativity blossom.

I hope your teachers see the beauty seared into your souls. You are whole, perfect, and complete the way you are, and when you walk into the schoolhouse, you bring what makes you unique. You are much more than well-behaved, well-mannered, well-spoken Black students. You are brilliant, good-looking, smart problem solvers.

You inspired me to write this book — to affirm all that is wonderful about you and to ensure you pass what makes you "beautifully you" to your children. I also wrote this book to increase the likelihood that your experiences in school don't dim the light shining through you.

I hope these words help you get to know me on a deeper level when you become adults. I want you to understand why your mom and I said and did certain things, specifically regarding your schooling. I want you to understand how much I obsessed over your school experiences because school systems, sometimes unknowingly, destroy students of color, crushing their spirits and confidence.

It is important that Black parents expose children to certain truths about schooling. The culmination of your experiences with your mom and me, particularly regarding your education, is a gift we give you, a primer on raising Black children to survive schooling and navigate this world.

Teachers, I hope reading this book helps you understand the gifts and unique experiences that my kids – and all Black children – bring to school. I hope that by reading about my experiences as a Black student, parent, and educator, you see Black students as whole human beings who deserve a high-quality education. I want this book to help us all address the unique struggles that Black students and families face navigating PreK–12 schooling.

Too many Black children suffer from substandard schooling and an overall lack of care from their teachers. Schools are removing people of color from curricula and library books; the number of Black and brown teachers is declining, and some educators' dispositions toward Black students are awful, negatively impacting the education that Black children receive.

Some Black children in your classes feel the world is stacked against them. Racial discrimination and insensitivity artificially and unnecessarily increase the difficulty of their lives. I hope my children's experiences with race-based unfairness are easier than mine and that they don't encounter race-based discrimination to the degree that I have.

Black parents who advocate for their kids' education sometimes face an uphill battle. I've had to persistently advocate for my children to get their free and appropriate public education. Unfortunately, my advocacy fell on deaf ears sometimes. I've witnessed educators in my children's schools refuse to teach students who are Black, Indigenous, and people of color and have low expectations for them. It's exhausting navigating the throes of school-based racial insensitivity, often causing racial battle fatigue, exhausting students and parents of color and affecting their relationships with schools.

My children had the benefit of growing up with two career educators as their mother and father. My kids' mom and I had to advocate, sometimes aggressively, to ensure our children's teachers did right by them. Unfortunately, every Black child doesn't have advocates at home, and some with advocates don't fully understand how schools work. I hope this book equips you with the knowledge, skills, and courage to be the advocate and teacher who Black students need.

Thank you for joining this journey captured in this book's pages. Thank you for being open to doing the work necessary to educate and advocate for Black students' right to a high-quality education and a positive school experience. It is a choice to do all you can to help Black children learn. Thank you for making the choice to be the kind of teacher that Black children need.

1

Black Students Need Teachers Who Understand That Education and Schooling Are Not the Same

Children, I want you to understand the difference between schooling and education. Schooling teaches students to pass tests and be successful at specific learning tasks. Education equips you to apply what you learn in school to the real world. Schooling trains, and sometimes compels, students to align to behavioral expectations that may not be in their best interests, while education helps students think critically and enhance who they are.

All of you have had awesome teachers; however, I'm not certain that those teachers taught you to explore and be curious about things that directly impact your well-being and the well-being of others. Zahra, the questions you've asked me about race clearly aren't being asked and answered in your classes. Zaire, your teachers have not always encouraged you to harness your energy and channel it in positive ways. Zamorah, even at seven years old, you ask me questions about race. Your school is one of the highest-achieving elementary schools in Las Vegas, but age-appropriate conversations about race, or at least about diversity, aren't happening regularly.

DOI: 10.4324/9781003529507-1

Yes, I'm pointing out how schooling has failed some Black students, but don't think I'm giving any of you a "pass" to fail. Though critical thinking and self-actualization don't appear to be cornerstones that consistently shine through in your school experiences, I still expect all of you to do well in school.

I expect all of you to master schooling, but don't assume that mastering schooling will prepare you for life, particularly since you are not routinely asked to be creative problem solvers. To be successful in life, you have to do more than memorize facts, earn good grades, and stay in the good graces of your teachers.

In life, you must use what you've learned to complete pragmatic tasks and solve practical challenges. This is why I'm so concerned that you all know how to think critically and solve real-world problems that you encounter. Being able to think critically will dramatically improve your quality of life. In fact, the ability to think critically is more predictive of positive life outcomes than raw intelligence and latent talent (Butler, 2017).

Look at facts and draw your own conclusions. Question things that don't make sense. Your life experiences are assets, so never hesitate to apply what you've learned outside of school to academic challenges. Teaching you how to apply what you know to real-world challenges should not be an add-on to your school curriculum; it should be integrated. You deserve an experience at school that will prepare you to make sense of our ever-changing world.

Help Black Students See Schooling As Useful

There is a difference between education and schooling. They are not the same. Education equips people with what they need to act in their best interests, pursue their goals, and self-actualize. Education enables people to apply what they learn to solve real-world problems. Anything other than that is schooling.

Schooling is the formal systems, structures, and processes students experience in a school such as curriculum standards, behavior expectations, and promotion requirements. Schooling provides students with ideas, experiences, knowledge, morals, and facts but doesn't necessarily teach students how to apply ideas, experiences, and knowledge in the real world. For instance, a student may know how to read but not be able to look at media with a critical eye and determine if a source is credible. A student may know math facts but not be able to apply their mathematical knowledge to tasks associated with financial literacy.

Schooling is also time bound. Grade school typically takes students 12 years to complete. It may take them another four or more years to earn a degree or credential. At some point, schooling ends, but education does not.

The education that Black children need must be relevant to them, help them understand their world, and help them pursue their dreams. The teachers Black students need understand this. They routinely teach in ways that enable Black students to connect what they learn in school to their lives outside of school. They encourage Black students to examine their world and connect their experiences to topics that surface naturally while learning the standards.

Black students learning science, for instance, should not be dissuaded from examining racially disproportionate exposure rates to air pollution, improper scientific experimentation, or inadequate health care if these topics naturally surface while learning state standards. All students should be allowed, indeed encouraged, to make connections between their lives and the state standards so that what they learn in school is meaningful, relevant, and applicable to them.

Too often when Black students make connections in class that intersect state standards with race, they are discouraged or not allowed to explore those topics. Some, and perhaps a large part, of this is because teachers don't know *how* to talk about race and don't know how to navigate such discussions. When Black students push too hard to have these sorts of conversations in classes where they are not welcomed, the students are too often labeled troublemakers.

Education vs. Schooling

Education	Schooling	Your Reflections
Empowers individuals to solve challenges they encounter	Focuses on imparting knowledge and Skills	In what ways does your school or classroom focus on "education?"
Can occur anywhere	Occurs at school	
Individualized Lifelong Process	Structured and Timebound	
Is not limited to formal institutions	Occurs in formal institutions	
Is not compulsory and is contextual	Often compulsory	

Figure 1.1 The differences between education and schooling.

Ensure Schooling Embraces Black Students

Ivan Illich, the author of *Deschooling Society*, wrote that schooling trains people to confuse grade advancement with education and teaching with actual learning. Illich believed that schools perpetuate societies' rituals, institutional morality, and the assimilation of people into institutionally acceptable behaviors (Illich, 1971). He believed schooling ultimately trains students to align with and accept a dominant culture's behavioral expectations of them.

Sometimes, cultural discontinuity exists between Black students' experiences outside of school and the expectations of their classroom teachers. More specifically, some Black students feel that schools ask them to "act White" and not display behavior typically associated with Black culture. This phenomenon is not surprising given that the majority of public schools in the US are run and taught by White educators. According to the National Center for Education Statistics, 80 percent of public school teachers in the US are White, while only six percent of teachers are Black (National Center for Education Statistics, 2024). The majority of K–12 students in public education are students of color and don't fit into public schools' dominant culture (National Center for Education Statistics, 2024).

When students don't fit into a dominant culture, as Illich said, schooling forces them to assimilate (Illich, 1971). If students don't comply or have difficulty adapting, they are often punished. A clear example of this was when Native American children were forced into boarding schools in the 1800s and early 1900s. They were punished for using their native languages and forced to abandon their religious beliefs, cultural behaviors, and traditional clothing and hair (Callimachi & Chischilly, 2021).

Similarly, Black students across the nation are being suspended and even expelled for wearing dreadlocks, afros, and other natural hairstyles (Aduayom & Locke, 2022). Dress code policies like these target Black students' identities and communicate that simply being who they are is disruptive and that they don't belong.

Black students who don't assimilate to school's White cultural norms are being pushed out of general education classes, as well. Due to racial bias, Black students are overrepresented in special education classes for learning disabilities and emotional and behavioral problems based on subjective placement, not actual need (Bronson, 2016).

Black students aren't only being pushed aside within their schools but systemically as well. A 2020 study from the National Center for Education Statistics' National Assessment of Educational Progress (NAEP) reported that "Black children are still relegated to separate and unequal schools" (Garcia, 2020). Public schools today are segregated by economic status, with some school districts even gerrymandering district lines to redirect low-income students to underperforming schools, which largely affects Black students (Crampton, 2018). The NAEP reported that 10 percent of White students attend high-poverty schools, whereas 60 percent of Black students do. When Black students are in segregated schools, they have lower standardized test scores, fewer resources, and less access to equal opportunities, widening the education gap.

Looking at the educational attainment of Black boys shows the consequences of prioritizing and forcing Black students to conform to the status quo over educating them. Of the roughly 320,000 African American boys who start ninth grade each year, 50 percent graduate high school, 15 percent go to a four-year college, and 2 percent attend moderately competitive colleges and universities (Aduayom & Locke, 2022). Blaming Black students for achievement gaps between them and their peers doesn't match the research. Schooling is failing Black boys.

> **Pause and Reflect**
>
> What can you do to increase Black students' feelings of belonging in your class? How can you make your Black students feel more welcome?
>
> _____
> _____
> _____

Affirm Your Black Students' Efforts and Interests

Unlike schooling, education affirms students and helps them enhance who they are. Having a diverse classroom library with Black protagonists, prioritizing underrepresented voices and perspectives in your teaching materials, and having posters of prominent Black people in your classroom are ways to affirm your Black students.

It is possible for students to go through school and not learn skills that equip them to succeed. It is a choice to make school useful to students, to educate students in ways that help them act in their best interests. This is why many teachers insist on making what they teach relevant to children and their diverse experiences so that their students can apply their knowledge outside of the classroom. Effective education must have practical application. Educators must ensure what they teach is relevant to students.

As a Howard University student, I was educated. I learned how to teach and lead in ways that would uplift African American children. Training to ensure academic excellence for Black children was not an add-on; it was the focal point of our training and development. Making educating Black children a focal point doesn't exclude the rest of your students; it benefits all students. In this book, I'll show you how you can educate your Black students and elevate the learning of all of your students.

Pause and Reflect

How do you affirm the interests and cultural background of your Black students?

_____

_____

_____

3–2–1 Chapter Reflection

Take a moment to reflect on the content of the chapter and what it means to you.

What are three important ideas from this chapter?

_____

_____

_____

What are two action steps you can take based on this chapter?

_____
_____
_____

What is one concept you would like to explore in more depth?

_____
_____
_____

References

Aduayom, D., & Locke, C. (2022, April 22). 6 kids speak out against hair discrimination. *The New York Times*. www.nytimes.com/2022/04/22/magazine/kids-hair-discrimination.html

Bronson, J. (2016). The overrepresentation of Black children in special education and the human right to education. In *Routledge eBooks* (pp. 205–218). https://doi.org/10.4324/9781315577401-13

Butler, H. A. (2017, February 5). Why do smart people do foolish things?. *Scientific American*. www.scientificamerican.com/article/why-do-smart-people-do-foolish-things/

Callimachi, R., & Chischilly, S. (2021, November 17). Lost lives, lost culture: The forgotten history of indigenous boarding schools. *The New York Times*. www.nytimes.com/2021/07/19/us/us-canada-indigenous-boarding-residential-schools.html

Crampton, D. (2018, October 19). *Gerrymandered school districts perpetuate segregation by keeping low-income students out, which is bad for economic growth*. Equitable Growth. https://equitablegrowth.org/gerrymandered-school-districts-perpetuate-segregation-by-keeping-low-income-students-out-which-is-bad-for-economic-growth/

Garcia, E. (2020, February 12). *Schools are still segregated, and Black children are paying a price*. Economic Policy Institute. Retrieved June 15, 2024, from www.epi.org/publication/schools-are-still-segregated-and-black-children-are-paying-a-price/

Illich, I. (1971). *Deschooling society*. Marion Boyars.

National Center for Education Statistics. (2021, May). *COE – characteristics of public school teachers*. Nces.ed.gov. https://nces.ed.gov/programs/coe/indicator/clr/public-school-teachers

National Center for Education Statistics. (2024). *Racial/ethnic enrollment in public schools*. Condition of Education. U.S. Department of Education, Institute of Education Sciences. https://nces.ed.gov/programs/coe/indicator/cge/racial-ethnic-enrollment

2

Black Students Succeed When Teachers Believe in Them

Zaire, I remember your first-grade teacher, Ms. Whitaker. She was an African American woman who was new to teaching and a former Division One basketball player who believed everyone could improve with practice. She wrote to your mom and me to introduce herself shortly after you were assigned to her class. She was the perfect teacher for you, especially after your kindergarten teacher, who was trifling, made you feel invisible and unworthy of attention by treating you as a problem, ignoring your raised hand, and checking in on every student except you during class.

You were an active kindergartener, Zaire, constantly moving and fidgeting. It took a lot of work for you to stay seated or be still at your desk. That didn't faze Ms. Whitaker. Instead of admonishing you, she worked closely with you to help you control your body's urges to move.

Ms. Whitaker built practices into the structure of her classroom that helped all students to self-regulate, focus, and communicate their needs to her. She gave you and your class frequent "brain breaks" that incorporated movement like Simon Says and one-minute dance breaks. She used "table incentives" that rewarded positive behaviors so that you and your peers held each other accountable for staying focused. Ms. Whitaker taught you and your class hand signals to let her know you needed to move. She was masterful. Whenever you had a bad day at school, Ms. Whitaker let your mom and I know the same day so we could redirect you.

Ms. Whitaker knew your interests outside of school and leveraged them to motivate you to master learning standards. She encouraged you to write stories about your family and favorite cartoon heroes when it was time to practice sentences. She also helped you understand math by connecting math concepts to your favorite video games and toys.

Ms. Whitaker helped students make friends, manage their emotions, and interact with each other respectfully. Zaire, you grew emotionally as a person in Ms. Whitaker's class. She had this activity named "Star Student" where all of the students in the class would write statements about what they liked about the "star student" and bind the statements in a book that she gave to parents. It was such a self-esteem builder. She would send us pictures of you through a teacher messaging app showing you doing your work and engaging in activities with your friends. You loved her, and she loved you. We loved her too, as parents.

Your mom and I had a birthday party for you at Chuck E. Cheese that year, and Ms. Whitaker showed up with a small gift. She understood the importance of her relationship with you and her relationship with your mom and me as your parents.

You were one of only a few African American boys in her class. Being school leaders at that time, your mom and I knew Ms. Whitaker's investment in you was as personal as it was professional. She got to know you and was invested in your growth and success. She knew and reviewed all of your formative achievement data with your mom and me quarterly. Your academic growth in Ms. Whitaker's class was astounding. She was perfect for you, Zaire. In fact, Ms. Whitaker was perfect for all the students blessed to be assigned to her class.

Ms. Whitaker won a "Heart of Education" award the year she had you in her class, an award only given to twenty out of over 14,000 teachers in Las Vegas. Your mom and I nominated her for the award. Ms. Whitaker was determined to ensure that all students learned in her class. As I write these words, Ms. Whitaker is the best teacher you have ever had. Ms. Whitaker is the kind of teacher that Black children need.

Set High Expectations and Black Students Will Strive to Meet Them

It is a well-documented fact that some teachers don't believe their Black students can achieve as well as their non-Black students (Gershenson et al., 2016). This negative bias becomes a self-fulfilling prophecy, contributing to the academic gap between Black students and their peers.

Black students are aware of when teachers lower their expectations for them. Black male high school students reported that compared with their non-Black peers, their teachers expected less of them academically and viewed them as disrespectful and dangerous rather than as critical thinkers (Allen, 2013). This contributes to Black students feeling out of place at school, diminishes their trust in and respect for their teachers, and for some, creates an internalized doubt in their own abilities.

In "I, Too, Am Harvard," a video by Ashante Bean that highlights the voices of Black Harvard College students, one student shared how as a Black person, his humanity and potential are rarely validated, saying, "Blackness to me is faith. Having faith in what you don't see because we, as a people, often don't see validation. For me, [being Black] is having faith that I am significant, I am valid, I am valuable, even though everything else is telling me that I'm not" (Ahsante the Artist, 2014).

The teachers Black students need set high expectations for all of their students and motivate all of their students to reach them. Your students will meet the expectations you have of them whether low or high. Some Black students may require scaffolds and support to master academic standards, just like your other students, but they *can* master them.

Pushing Black students to achieve shows that you care. Present challenging ideas and texts to your students. Push them to think about things outside of their experiences. Encourage them to form opinions and support their views with evidence.

Believing students can succeed is a "love language" in and of itself. Teachers like Ms. Whitaker don't accept failure from their kids. Instead, they set high expectations for them, all of them. When teachers do this, their students sit up straighter, hold their heads up a little higher, and thrive. When you hold high expectations for your students, they will do the same.

Getting Black students to meet high expectations is not exclusively a result of raising the bar on achievement and simply telling students to reach it. In practice, creating the conditions for Black students to master academic standards looks like many things, such as monitoring and sharing your students' academic growth, knowing when to push Black students and when to give leeway, seeing your Black students' strengths, and making their learning relevant.

Celebrate Black Students' Academic Growth So Students Can See Their Improvement

Make the process and pathway to mastering standards overt. As Ms. Whitaker did, empower your students to take an interest in their academic improvement and make tracking academic growth a community norm. Ms. Whitaker displayed growth charts on her wall, and her students graphed their academic progress in their notebooks regularly, allowing them to monitor their academic performance and take responsibility for their academic growth. Tracking academic growth was so firmly ingrained in her classroom culture that all of her students knew their performance targets and progress toward reaching them.

Having your students track their academic growth is a powerful practice, and so is reflection. Include check-in questions like "What about your academic progress are you proud of?" and "What learning target can you use more support in?" Not only will questions like these increase your students' self-awareness, ownership, and pride in their learning journey, but they will also show you where your students need more support and highlight academic accomplishments that you can celebrate. You can send a letter home or call your students' parents and let them know that you are proud of their child for their growth in meeting [fill in the blank] learning target and their ability to recognize where they need support and to ask for help.

It's also important to let your students know that you acknowledge their academic growth and the effort they're putting in. A simple note recognizing and celebrating their progress can have a big impact.

Ms. Whitaker also shared students' growth charts at parent-teacher conferences. The running record of Ms. Witaker's students' improvement gave parents insight into their children's academic performance and what they needed to do at home to help their children reach their growth goals. Hold regular meetings with your students' parents to review their child's growth, and help them understand how they can support their child's learning at home. This is also a great opportunity to let parents know that you're proud of their child's growth and the work they're putting in.

> **Pause and Reflect**
> How do you promote a culture of high expectations in your classroom? How do you celebrate students' academic growth?
> _____
> _____
> _____

Be Mindful of When to Push and Pull Your Black Students Toward Academic Growth

There's an ebb and flow to learning. The teachers Black students need know when to push and pull students to get them to the proverbial "there." It used to be a popular opinion that it was *always* good to push students academically, but the increase in the number of children who struggle with anxiety, depression, and stress-related health issues makes it clear that teachers must be mindful of how they push students. Otherwise, you risk pushing students into a "survival state" defined by stress, trauma, or fear of falling short of academic expectations (Table 2.1). When the brain enters a survival state, traversing emotionally tough moments becomes the priority, not learning. Relaxed brains learn better (Hobson, 2020).

Creating a classroom environment where Black students feel cared for is vital. It's in these environments where students feel safe to be pushed. Relying on your relationships and your understanding of your Black students as individuals will help you create these types of learning environments for them.

Being socially aware can help you deepen your relationships with Black students so that you can create learning environments where they feel safe to be academically pushed. Being socially aware means being empathetic to the needs, inequalities, and injustices diverse groups experience and understanding how your actions affect them.

To develop social awareness, seek to understand your Black students' perspectives and understand that Black students' perspectives can be diverse. Learn about the social issues that impact your Black students and their families, and perhaps join community organizations working to address those issues. When your Black students see that you're making an effort to learn about their lives and understand their

Table 2.1 Pressures Black Students Can Experience that Can Impede Learning

Causes of Academic or Personal Pressure	Description	Have you ever experienced stress as a result of these factors? If yes, please explain
Pressure from self	When students are hyper-focused on their academic performance, they may internalize pressure they experience.	
Pressure from parents or guardians	Parents and guardians sometimes place extreme pressure on their students to excel in school. This places extra pressure on students.	
Pressure from poor organization or poor time management	Students' time management or organization skills are developing during their school-aged years. Students sometimes feel pressure when they experience difficulty managing their time or responsibilities.	
Pressure from assessments	Tests, exams, and any kind of assessment can put a lot of pressure on young people to perform well.	
Pressure from extreme competitiveness	Students' pressure on themselves to perform academically sometimes turns into extreme competitiveness with their peers, or even within themselves.	
Pressure from perceived racial discrimination, racial abuse, or race-based unfairness	Black students know when their academic work is measured differently than their non-black peers and when their classroom contributions are not regarded. This causes Black students to experience anxiety and pressure.	
Pressure of being a victim of race-based school police violence against them	Students in schools with officers sometimes feel a fear of being targeted for officer-involved violence or entanglements. This creates pressure for Black students to behave in ways they think won't trigger unwanted attention from law enforcement.	

perspectives, they'll see that as a sign that you care about them, and that will help lay a foundation for trust.

Active listening is an important step in building social awareness. Actively listen and pay attention to social cues that communicate your Black students' feelings about learning materials, class discussions, and classroom and school-wide structures. Pay attention to how your Black students' facial expressions change in response to words or actions. Recognize when your Black students communicate boredom or restlessness through fidgeting. Notice when your Black students' bodies tense up because they are stressed or upset. Recognize when your Black students display clenched teeth, tight lips, flared nostrils, or frowning because they are angry. When you pay attention to your Black students' social cues, you'll start to understand the meaning of their voice intonations, body language, and verbal and nonverbal cues. This will help you identify and meet your Black students' needs, deepen your relationships with them, and know when to push and pull them toward academic growth.

School-appropriate self-disclosure is another important part of building relationships with your Black students. When you share information about yourself, research shows that it encourages others to do the same. Self-disclosure creates stronger emotional bonds, increases trust, and creates a sense of belonging (Cherry, 2023). These are the qualities that you want in your relationships with your students so you know when to push and when to pull academically.

Share your interests outside of the classroom with your students. Let them know that you have a life outside of being their teacher. In addition to factual disclosure, sharing your likes and dislikes and your thoughts on your favorite school-appropriate movie or television show you like, it's important to also emotionally disclose in order to more easily develop empathy and trust in your relationships with your students ("Self-Disclosure," 2024).

Share your feelings, hopes, ambitions, and fears with your students, but make sure what you share is appropriate. Share what you struggled with most as a student and who inspired you. Don't share how the teacher across the hallway is frustrating you. Making a mistake and admitting it can be vulnerable, but it can show your awareness that we are all learners. No one has all the answers. If you planned a lesson that you've realized is a complete flop, tell your students.

Self-disclosure must be a reciprocal process. You need to make space for your Black students to self-disclose as well. Ask them about their interests outside of class. Give assignments that allow students to share about themselves and connect what they are learning to their lives. Incorporate community-building activities in your class that allow students to share about themselves and how they feel. Have morning meetings every morning that facilitate relationship building with you and among students. You could take five minutes at the start of class for students to share their roses and thorns, one positive and one negative thing. Sharing can be low stakes (e.g., "I'm tired") to higher stakes (e.g., "My cousin got in a car accident, and I'm worried"). Of course, enlist the support of a school counselor if a student discloses something concerning.

When you create relationships with your Black students based on trust, they will trust that what you do is in their best interest, and when you push them academically, they will put in the effort to meet your expectations.

In order to feel safe in their learning environment, your Black students need to know that your care and support are not contingent on their behavior or academic performance. Caring about students as individuals breaks down barriers that may exist. Be caring without conditions. Ensure you separate discipline matters from relationship matters. Classroom management and relationship building are two different activities. Don't define students by their behavior.

To help push your students toward mastering standards, create an environment where mistakes aren't punished but a part of the process and where academic curiosity is rewarded. Create scaffolds to help when needed. Teach a series of mini-lessons that build on each other and progressively build students' understanding of academic concepts. Model how to complete academic tasks. Use think-alouds to teach students how to process information and gain a deeper understanding of academic concepts. Scaffold instruction by explaining concepts in multiple ways. Incorporate visual aids to build background knowledge of concepts and front-load academic vocabulary. When students find themselves on the right academic path, push them to keep going. Encourage them every step of the way, mindful of their needs as individual learners.

> **Pause and Reflect**
> What can you do in your class to communicate to Black students that you care about them and their futures?
>
> _____
> _____
> _____

When you present content, your emotional state is as important as the pedagogy you use to teach it. It's important to be calm, clear, and patient when presenting content so your Black students will be receptive to being pushed academically. This is true for all students, but Black students in particular are more prone to being dismissed or disproportionately disciplined by their teachers, making a calm, clear, and patient presence even more impactful. Black students know when teachers are unnecessarily mean or hostile toward them, and it undermines the possibility of a positive relationship.

Being clear means not only being clear in terms of explaining assignments and tasks but also being clear in mind and being fully present. It is important for you to foster a calm atmosphere in your classroom and refrain from being a "reactionary yeller." Remain calm when explaining or reinforcing academic expectations to students, particularly students with academic difficulties. Consistently be patient with students, and give them time to figure things out, acclimate, and adjust.

See Your Students' Strengths and Potential So They Can See Them, Too

My son was a kid who felt a constant need to move. Controlling his body was a challenge for him. When Ms. Whitaker saw Zaire's constant need to move, she didn't punish him or the behavior. Instead, she helped him manage and redirect his energy. Sometimes, she allowed Zaire to stand up while she taught. She didn't reprimand Zaire when he didn't sit on his bottom at his desk. Ms. Whitaker didn't let Zaire's need to move define him or disrupt his learning. She saw Zaire as the passionate, intelligent, and curious boy he was, and she helped him not just control his body but also grow academically and emotionally.

You may have a student in your class like Zaire, who needs help staying seated, or a student who sleeps in class, gets distracted easily, or talks when listening is better. Too often, students who exhibit these behaviors are labeled disruptive. Their needs get dismissed, and they get left behind. They start to be seen as a problem.

Students' quirks or mischievous behaviors don't necessarily reflect their willingness or ability to learn. There could be a thousand reasons behind your students' behavior: not having access to food or a safe place to sleep, the stress of caregiving for siblings or working to support their family, being neglected at home, or perhaps being bullied by peers. Your Black students in particular may have had teachers before you who didn't believe in them or support them. Your Black students may think, "Why should I respect what my teacher says if they don't respect or care about me?"

Don't let challenging behaviors limit your perception of what your students can achieve. If you have a student whose talking is disruptive, for example, meet with them one on one, let them know how talking during instruction negatively impacts the learning environment, and help them find ways to positively redirect their need to talk. Avoid shaming them as a behavior modification technique, as shaming students tarnishes your relationships with them. Give them roles in facilitating group discussions, create pair-and-share activities where they can leverage their need to talk to benefit their learning, and have them set goals on how they can constructively use their voice.

Like Ms. Whitaker communicated with Zaire's mom and me when he struggled sitting still in class, communicate with your students' parents on the days they struggle. That way, you and your students' families can partner to help them succeed. Equally as important, let parents know when their kids have great days so they can celebrate them and reinforce the positive behavior. The teachers Black students need don't just do these things for African American students. They do this for all of their students.

Make Learning Relevant to Keep Black Students Engaged

The teachers Black students need ensure that Black students see positive representations of themselves in the classroom curriculum. Too often, school districts and officials regulate or even censor the exploration of race, gender, and sexual orientation in schools because discussing these topics makes some people uncomfortable.

Suppose you omit discussions about race that naturally surface when teaching academic standards. In that case, you communicate to your students of color that their identity makes you uncomfortable and that they and their experiences are not welcome in the classroom. When students are not allowed to connect the curriculum to their everyday lives and apply what they learn to their worlds, their motivation to learn diminishes, especially when they're made to feel that they don't belong in the classroom.

All students deserve to feel like they belong in their classrooms, and too many Black students don't. Let your Black students know that you value them for who they are as people. Let them know that they belong in your classroom and that it's safe for them to be their authentic selves. In order to achieve this, your Black students need to see themselves represented in the curriculum. They need to know that it's okay to talk about their experiences and that the classroom is a safe space to connect what they are learning to their lives.

Be courageous. As long as your students share their thoughts and wonderings about race respectfully, and appropriate to your school and their ages, allow and facilitate the discussions. There are many ways to make classroom content relevant to Black students. Use texts with African American protagonists and stories set in African American communities when teaching students how to identify and explain literary devices in grade-appropriate texts. Use poems written by African American authors when teaching students how word choice appeals to the senses and suggests mood, tone, and style. Let students studying science use the scientific method to explore why some diseases, such as high blood pressure or sickle cell, disproportionately affect individuals of color. Allow students in statistics class to compute the probability of natural disasters or disparate resources and how they impact people living in different cities or zip codes. Teach students about the rich culture of Africa in social studies lessons.

Classrooms should be a marketplace of ideas. However, be careful that your facilitation of discussions about race remains neutral and that you don't let your biases dictate the discussion. Students must be free to form their own opinions in grade-level-appropriate and age-appropriate ways. The teachers Black students need help make classroom instruction relevant to them and all of their students.

> **Pause and Reflect**
> Please describe an assignment you gave students that Black students found culturally relevant to them. If you have not assigned Black students culturally relevant assignments, what barriers are you experiencing? Please share.
>
> _____
> _____
> _____

3–2–1 Chapter Reflection

Take a moment to reflect on the content of this chapter and what it means to you.

What are three important ideas from this chapter?
_____
_____
_____

What are two action steps you can take based on this chapter?
_____
_____
_____

What is one concept you would like to explore in more depth?

_____

_____

_____

References

Allen, Q. (2013). "They Think minority means lesser than" Black middle-class sons and fathers resisting microaggressions in the school. *Urban Education, 48*, 171–197. https://doi.org/10.1177/0042085912450575

Bean, A. (Producer). (2024, February 28). *I, too, am Harvard.* www.youtube.com/watch?v=uAMTSPGZRiI

Cherry, K. (2023, September 5). How self-disclosure impacts relationships. *Verywell Mind.* www.verywellmind.com/how-does-self-disclosure-influence-relationships-4122387

Gershenson, S., Holt, S. B., & Papageorge, N. W. (2016). Who believes in me? The effect of student – teacher demographic match on teacher expectations. *Economics of Education Review, 52*, 209–224. https://doi.org/10.1016/j.econedurev.2016.03.002

Hobson, N. (2020, December 20). The neural underpinnings of how stress interferes with learning and memory. *Psychology Today.* www.psychologytoday.com/us/blog/ritual-and-the-brain/201804/why-your-brain-stress-fails-learn-properly

Self-disclosure. (2024). Connecting with honest, personal communication. www.mindtools.com/agr7y2v/self-disclosure

3

Don't Let Microaggressions Define Black Students' Classroom Experiences

Zahra, your kindergarten teacher loved you. Her name was Ms. Jenkins. She pushed you to grow as a student and person. I remember you complaining about Ms. Jenkins because she made you do assignments over, sometimes several times if they were not your best work. Ms. Jenkins set high expectations for you.

Searching for the best educational experience for you, Zahra, we applied to get you into Northern Academy of the Arts Elementary School for first grade, a lottery-based magnet school. Northern Academy was THE performing arts school. You got accepted, and you were thrilled to attend.

You went into first grade excited to learn, Zahra. When you entered Northern Academy, your test scores in English and math were in the 90th percentile. By the end of first grade, your achievement levels had dropped precipitously, and they didn't improve in your second-grade classroom. Your mom and I realized that the culturally affirming foundation of trust and high expectations that you had experienced with Ms. Jenkins was missing from your school experience this year.

Your third-grade teacher's name was Ms. Cunningham. She was a nice lady, but ineffective. Time she could have used to build relationships with you and your classmates, she instead used to openly complain about Northern Academy's principal, Mr. Sanford. You made it clear that you didn't like when Ms. Cunningham did this. One day, you came home visibly frustrated with Ms. Cunningham; she had burst into tears at her desk after angrily complaining about how Mr. Sanford was changing things at Northern Academy School of the Arts.

"I'm tired of Ms. Cunningham saying stuff about Mr. Sanford," you said. "Mr. Sanford is nice and always asks us what we're learning. I don't think it's professional for her to talk bad about Mr. Sanford." Because you are the child of two career educators, you knew precisely what comprised professional behavior in schools.

Zahra, you got so frustrated with Ms. Cunningham that, without any prompting, you told Mr. Sanford what Ms. Cunningham was saying about him in class. You felt comfortable going to Mr. Sanford because you knew that Mr. Sanford cared about you. He showed interest in you and asked you questions about things you were learning. That trust in him made you feel safe to communicate your needs to him. Ms. Cunningham was not at Northern Academy the following year.

Your relationship with your kindergarten teacher was special, Zahra. That was not the case with Ms. Cunningham. She doubted your intelligence and set low expectations for you, a microaggression that Black students experience too often.

When you have your own kids, Zahra, advocate for them to have teachers like Ms. Jenkins. Strong teacher–student relationships are vital to the academic success of Black students and are integral to preventing, addressing, and learning from microaggressions.

What Are Microaggressions?

Microaggressions are actions or words that are discriminatory or derogatory toward someone based on their socioeconomic status, religion, gender, gender identity or expression, sexual orientation, disability, nationality, race, ethnicity, or other characteristics associated with a particular group of people. Microaggressions invalidate a group's identity, are derogatory or dismissive of individuals' experiences, and have a harmful and lasting impact on those who experience them (*The Harmful Effects of Microaggressions | Duke Today*, 2022).

These commonplace behavioral, verbal, and environmental slights and discriminatory acts are often subtle, and people are often unaware when they commit them, making microaggressions insidious. An example of microaggressive behavior is when someone tells a Black person that they "don't see color" and "see" them the same way as they see everyone else. To tell a Black person this is to tell them you don't see them at all or anything about their cultural experiences that makes them unique. While someone who says this microaggression may be well-intentioned, their comment diminishes Black people's unique experiences and communicates that the things that make Black people beautifully unique don't matter.

Help Prevent Microaggressions in the Classroom by Being Aware of Your Unconscious Biases

To prevent microaggressions in your classroom, you must recognize and reflect on your own biases and behaviors. Knowing more about yourself – your biases and worldview – will make it easier for you to catch your limiting beliefs and will make you less likely to commit microaggressive behaviors. Everyone has biases; if you have a brain, you have biases. The key is to be mindful of them so that your interactions in your classroom don't trigger microaggressive, biased responses.

It's important to recognize and manage your biases, as well as seek to understand how your actions can trigger students to behave in ways that are counterproductive to learning and the classroom culture that you want to create. Seek to understand how your personal biases, values, and beliefs influence your behaviors. Decide to interrupt your biases when they surface. Make a conscious decision to take your thoughts off autopilot so you can recognize biased behavior and interrupt it. This will help you from unknowingly engaging in microaggressive behaviors toward your students. One way to become aware of your own biases is to take Project Implicit's race implicit association test (*Take a Test*, n.d.). Project Implicit is a nonprofit that researches implicit bias. After taking the test, reflect on your results.

Forming friendships with diverse people will also help you to become aware of and lessen your unconscious biases. Research has shown that people who interact socially with people of another race feel more anxiety, stress, and a sense of threat than they do when they socialize with their own race. When people are friends with others of different races, it decreases their stress when they are with interracial groups, and it decreases their prejudices (Suttie, 2016).

If you are friends with diverse people, it will most likely increase your comfort level and decrease the implicit biases you may have with your diverse students, enabling you to connect more with your Black students. Your friendships (inside and outside of school) will also model to your students that interracial and cross-group friendships are okay to form, creating a classroom culture that's more receptive to cross-group friendships and where microaggressions are less likely to occur.

Another thing you can do to become aware of your implicit biases is to privately track your interactions with your students (Wamsted, 2021). Use a clipboard to track them for a month. Track which students you discipline, whose raised hands you call on, which students you cold-call to ask questions, and which students you joke with and talk to about their interests outside of the classroom.

Also track how you are feeling in class. Are you tired? Are you anxious? You may discover that you give in to biases when you're under pressure, stressed, or tired. When tired, you may realize that you do not ask a particular group of students about their interests outside of school or welcome them to share them in class. When stressed, you may find that you discipline a group of students disproportionately. These data are starting points for further reflection.

Comprise a list of students you can make a point to have conversations with. Identify students you will be mindful to call on when they raise their hands. Determine if there is a group of students you discipline disproportionately. Be mindful of how stress and fatigue influence interactions with your students.

Simply being aware of your emotions and behavior patterns is helpful. If you know that you discipline or argue with a group of students disproportionately when you're stressed, being aware of that fact can help you to be more mindful of how you interact with those students when you are stressed. You can start to check yourself if you notice that you're treating a group of students unfairly, apologize, and then continuously work to change your behavior. Apologizing to a student can feel vulnerable, but it's also a powerful step in building trust and repairing harm.

Also, take note of what triggers your feelings. You might notice that you're more stressed during parent–teacher conferences. Knowing that, during parent–teacher conference week, you can start your classes with a grounding meditation, a few deep breaths, or some type of brain break to help you feel more grounded. When you know what triggers your stress, anxiety, or frustration at school, you can plan ways to mitigate it so that you can be more present with yourself and your students and less likely to commit microaggressions against your students.

It's helpful to pay attention to teachers who excel at getting diverse students to learn, as well. Do what they do? Ask them how they interrupt hate and bias and incorporate their strategies and routines into your classroom and teaching.

> **Pause and Reflect**
>
> What steps have you taken to become more aware of unconscious biases you may have? Please share.
>
> _____
> _____
> _____

Use Your Classroom Management Toolbox to Prevent Microaggressions

Black students are disproportionately disciplined due to racial biases, cultural gaps, and misunderstandings. Sometimes, school personnel believe students *should* know certain behavioral expectations without being told, but implicit academic, social, and cultural norms valued by school staff sometimes don't align with the behavioral norms in students' homes and their lives outside of school. It is not always willful disobedience when students misbehave in class; sometimes they don't understand behavioral expectations. Invalidating students' cultural norms and punishing them for it is a microaggressive behavior that can be prevented by increasing your awareness of how you implement your classroom management strategies.

You know the behavioral norms in your class that will create the learning environment you want for your students. Preventing microaggressions in how you manage your classroom is a combination of teaching students your classroom norms and learning their needs so that they can learn. On day one, create clear classroom behavior norms and expectations *with* students. It is easier to hold students accountable for expectations they helped create than for those created by others. Clear academic, social, and behavioral expectations empower students to make informed choices and help mitigate disruptive behavior. Refer to the subsection "Address Microaggressions in Your Classroom" for more on how to create classroom norms with students.

There is a hidden curriculum of unspoken behavioral expectations that are widely known by some students but not widely known by others (Alsubaie, 2015): Teach that hidden curriculum. For instance, it may be an unspoken expectation that students are only allowed to speak when they raise their hand and a teacher calls on them. Not all students come to school knowing what behaviors are expected of them so it's important to teach the hidden curriculum.

Also, however, hold students accountable for their behaviors. Holding students accountable for their behavior is not synonymous with being mean, inconsiderate, insensitive, or divvying out punishment. Punishment focuses students' attention on the consequences they suffer rather than on the impacts of their behavior on their classroom environment and peers. Punishment also creates an external locus of control rather than helping students take responsibility for their behavior choices. Forcing kids to write behavior sentences, making them stand in a corner, taking away recess, or giving them a timeout as responses to poor behavior can erode relationships between students and teachers.

Consequences can be a part of holding students accountable, but students also need to understand how their behavior negatively impacts their peers and disrupts learning, including for themselves. They also need to be taught the positive behaviors you expect from them.

Teach the replacement behaviors you are seeking from students. For replacement behaviors to be effective, they need to be taught. It's important to know the reason why your student is not listening or acting out so you can teach them the replacement behavior that best meets their needs.

If a student talks out of turn or blurts out answers instead of raising their hand, they could be seeking attention. Plan activities that involve talking so your student's need to talk can be productive. Think-pair-share, jigsaw, interviews, role playing, group discussions, and debates are all ways to utilize talking for learning. Explain to your student the difference between productive talking and disruptive talking and how their talking can be a strength when used productively. Give examples.

Let your student know the behavior that you want them to do; they can raise their hand if they want to answer a question or if they need help. When you acknowledge them for speaking out of turn, remind them of the consequences for speaking out of turn, and remind them to raise their hand.

Reinforce the positive behavior. When your student raises their hand, praise them. Smile at them or thank them for raising their hand. Praise other students who raise their hands to model and reinforce the positive behavior you want in your class, and if it's not too disruptive, ignore the behavior you don't want. When students blurt out answers, don't respond.

Ignore minor, attention-seeking behaviors so they don't inadvertently reinforce inappropriate behavior. Ignore whining, tattling, pouting, fidgeting, and mild behavioral meltdowns. Consistently ignoring problematic behavior diminishes it, although remember that when you ignore behavior, it tends to increase for a while before it stops. Also remember that ignoring minor, poor behavior is not the same as ignoring a child.

Use calm, subtle ways to approach students who are misbehaving or off task. Even the best teachers can sometimes lose their cool, so don't punish yourself for having a human reaction to tough situations. Teaching is a stressful job. Know that responding to a student reactively tends to increase their negative behavior. Students know and respond to your tone of voice and body language. When you know which students trigger you and what situations trigger you, create a plan to help you destress. For example, before approaching a student who frequently misbehaves and gets on your nerves, take an intentional, deep breath.

Use proximity to subtly let students know when they are misbehaving or off task. Have you ever walked toward students who were talking and as you neared them, they stopped? This is called proximity interference. Sometimes simply moving near students who are off-task or misbehaving will encourage them to stop the behavior. You can also use proximity to prevent misbehavior from students before it starts. If proximity alone doesn't work, calmly approach off-task students and quietly explain to them that they are being disruptive. You can also develop silent signals with your students, such as hand gestures, to let students know they are off task and that you need them to refocus.

Factor in breaks so students aren't required to work for long periods without losing focus or getting distracted. Generally, elementary students need a three- to five-minute break after focused learning for 10 to 15 minutes, and secondary students need a break after 20 to 30 minutes (Terada, 2022). Short brain breaks help students self-regulate, reduce stress, and increase focus and productivity (Willis, 2016). Research also shows that breaks help to consolidate learning and help prevent cognitive fatigue (Terada, 2022). Taking a brain break can be as simple as having students stretch, draw whatever they want with their non-dominant hand, or playing Simon Says.

Black students lose a significant amount of trust in school and educators by the seventh grade when they become more aware of being unfairly disciplined by their teachers due to racial bias, according to a 2017 study published in the *Child Development Journal* (Yeager et al., 2017). Many Black students come to school knowing that the school system, the curriculum, the policies, and their classes weren't created with them in mind, which creates a sense of alienation instead of belonging. Black students walk into their classrooms with the expectation that they'll experience microaggressions regularly. This all contributes to a gap in trust. The teachers Black students need break the cycle of distrust. Reflect on how your implicit bias may seep into classroom management strategies and how you implement them. Take the time to get to know your Black students and how to meet their needs. Do all you can to maintain positive relationships with students while helping them adhere to behavioral expectations.

Ways Black Students Experience Microaggressions in Schools

Unfortunately, it is not uncommon for African American students to experience microaggressions at school, making it harder for them to manage school life. Yolanda Flores Niemann, a professor of psychology at the University of North Texas, captured students' perspectives about microaggressions in a video titled "Microaggressions in the Classroom" (Focused Arts Media Education, 2017). One Black student shared that after she told her teacher she wanted a career as a psychiatry, her teacher told her she wasn't smart enough to achieve her career aspirations: "That's too hard for you," her teacher said. "Have you ever thought about being a nurse practitioner? Nurse practitioners in psychiatry, they make a lot of money, too. Why would you go to med school?" With tears in her eyes, the student told the researcher, "Sometimes, somebody might feel like they can't make it. And when you continue to tell them that, it does hurt."

A Black student who played sports shared how one of his peers didn't see him as a Black person because he was smart. A non-Black peer told him, 'Yes, you're athletic, but you do your work, you're smart, so I don't really know if you're Black." Another student in the video was told by his non-Black peer, "You're the least scary Black guy I've ever met." He shared that he and his Black male peers deliberately behave in ways to make themselves appear less threatening to others to avoid microaggressive behaviors toward them. He said Black students change how they dress, speak, and walk in public spaces so others don't see them as threatening. "It's sad you have to make sure you let people know you're not a threat, and that's the objective," another Black male student shared.

> **Pause and Reflect**
>
> Do Black students experience race-based microaggressions in your class? Please explain. Do you experience race-based microaggressions at your school? Please share.
>
> _____
>
> _____
>
> _____

Microaggressions Affect Black Students Negatively

Microaggressions hurt Black students and negatively shape their school experiences. According to the Education Commission of the States, a nonpartisan nonprofit that supports education policy leaders, teachers' expectations of their students are the most significant in-school factor that dictates student success (Loewus, 2020). Teachers' expectations of Black students impact the academic rigor of their instruction and how they support Black students academically. The teachers Black students need are mindful of this.

It is not uncommon for Black students to feel they have few meaningful interactions with adults in schools, feel invisible to adults, and believe their teachers do not care about them or their futures (Allen, 2010) (Andrews, 2023). There is a body of research that provides insight into why Black students feel this way. For instance, the US Department of Education's National Center for Education Statistics conducted a study where they asked high school teachers how far they thought their 10th-grade students would go in school (Gershenson & Papageorge, 2017). Teachers in the study believed 58 percent of their White students and only 37 percent of their Black students would earn a four-year degree.

Table 3.1 Types of Microaggression

Type	Explanation	Have you experienced this type of microaggression? Please explain.
Verbal	A verbal microaggression is a comment or question that is hurtful or stigmatizing to a marginalized group or person, for example saying, "You're so smart for a woman."	
Behavioral	This involves behaving in a way that is discriminatory or otherwise hurtful to a marginalized person or group, for example, when a waiter or bartender ignores a transgender person and instead serves a cisgender person, someone whose biological sex matches their gender identity.	
Environmental	An environmental microaggression is when a subtle discrimination occurs within society, for example, when a college campus only has buildings named after white people.	

Table 3.2 Classifications of Microaggressions

Classification	Explanation	Have you experienced this type of microaggression? Please explain.
Microassaults	This is when a person intentionally behaves in a discriminatory way. An example is saying a racial epithet, displaying a swastika, or telling a racist joke, then saying, "I was just joking."	
Microinsults	This is a comment or action that is unintentionally discriminatory. For example, saying to an Indian doctor, "Your people must be so proud."	
Microinvalidations	This is when a person's comment invalidates or undermines the experiences of a marginalized group. An example would be a White person telling a Black person that "Racism does not exist in today's society."	

The power of teachers' expectations is formidable. Researchers tracked the students in the study to test teachers' assumptions. Forty-nine percent of White students in the study and 29 percent of Black students earned a four-year degree (Gershenson & Papageorge, 2017). Teachers' low expectations of Black students shaped their Black students' realities, becoming a self-fulfilling prophecy. It makes sense. Why would any student want to learn from someone who doesn't believe in them or their future?

Black students are also unfairly disciplined by their teachers due to racial bias. The US Department of Education Office for Civil Rights found that for every four White students suspended from schools, 14 Black students are suspended (Civil Rights Data Collection: Data Snapshot, 2014). Black girls are disciplined more than any other race of girls and more than White and Asian boys.

Repeated race-based microaggressive behavior can traumatize Black students. Trauma can trigger the fight, flight, or freeze response, which shuts down the part of the brain that controls attention, memory, and learning (Desautels, 2016). Many students who exhibit signs of trauma in the classroom are written off as bad students for being forgetful, missing deadlines, or having emotional outbursts, instead of being supported (Todd, 2021). As a result, they fall behind academically, widening the achievement gap. The teachers Black students need are mindful of the impacts of race-based microaggressive behavior and do all they can to ensure it does not negatively impact their Black students' health, well-being, and academic performance.

Common Microaggressions in the Classroom and How to Prevent Them

The teachers Black students need understand that race-based discrimination and microaggressions can affect Black students acutely, and they support their African American students who may be suffering from the trauma associated with them. Being aware of common microaggressions is the first step in protecting your Black students from them.

It's important to be aware of common microaggressions so that you can avoid them and guard your Black students against microaggressive behavior in your classroom. First, reflect on how you may be contributing to microaggressions in the classroom and change your own microaggressive behaviors.

Remember the data you collected about how you interact with your students and any unconscious bias it revealed. Are you not pushing your Black students to meet high expectations as you do for other students? If that's something you uncovered when collecting data about your own biases, start telling your Black students that you believe they can meet your high expectations and support them to get there.

Do you give nicknames to students whose names are difficult for you to pronounce? Instead, take the time to learn how to pronounce their names correctly. Names are an important part of your students' identities. When you call a student by their name, it helps them feel seen. When you don't, it's microaggressive behavior that signals to your students that you don't care about them.

It's also important to reflect on the content you teach, how you teach it, and its impact on your Black students. When teaching content about Black people, like slavery and the Civil Rights movement, or discussing books that explore Black cultural experiences, don't single out your Black students and ask for "their perspective as a Black person." This is a microaggressive behavior that many Black students expressed frustration with Ahsante Bean's video "I, Too, Am Harvard." One student in the video shared:

> When you're in class, and you're the only Black kid, and the issue of race comes up, everyone looks to you as if you're about to speak for your race. It's frustrating

because you would hope that people would understand that there are all different types of Black people, and Black people don't all have the same opinions about the same issues. So I'm always tempted to hold back and not say anything because I don't want to feel like they're going to take what I say as representative of everyone.

(Bean [Ahsante the Artist], 2014)

Teaching only about Black people's experiences during Black History Month is also a microaggressive behavior. By not including Black authors, historians, and experiences in the content you teach, you're communicating to all of your students that their experiences and lives are not valuable or worthy of learning about. This communicates to your Black students that they and their experiences don't belong in your classroom.

Be intentional about what you teach when teaching about Black people's experiences. If you teach history, do you only teach about slavery or Martin Luther King Jr. and Rosa Parks? When students are only educated about Black struggle, a narrow perception is created of Black culture and lives that impacts how non-Black students perceive their Black peers and how Black students perceive themselves and what they're capable of. It's important to also teach about Black success.

For instance, when teaching world history, your students can learn about Charles Richard Drew, an American surgeon whose research in blood transfusions led him to develop large-scale blood banks during World War II. When teaching themes, motifs, and literary devices, you can use "Sonny's Blues," a short story by James Baldwin, one of the greatest writers of the 20th century. Your students need to see examples of Black people thriving and contributing to society in a variety of roles so that non-Black students can have a wider view of Black people's experiences and so that Black students can see more examples of what they can grow up to be. By not including perspectives from Black figures in your content, you're communicating to your students that Black people's contributions to society aren't significant enough to learn about and that they don't matter.

Address Microaggressions in Your Classroom

Your classroom is a community made up of many students, so you can't always prevent microaggressions from happening. You can, however, anticipate how microaggressions may arise and plan ways to address them.

One way to mitigate microaggressions in your classroom is to create an anti-racist classroom culture that promotes respect, belonging, and open communication. Being anti-racist means that you take action to counter racial prejudice and systemic racism and promote racial equality. "Shouting down" prejudice has virtually nothing to do with being "woke" and everything to do with being kind, caring, inclusive, and concerned about every students' learning. Having frequent conversations about understanding, acceptance, and respect with your students helps create an anti-racist classroom. Creating inclusive classrooms is an ongoing effort, and frequent whole-class conversations such as these will keep the classroom community focused on behaving in unbiased ways.

Start by creating classroom norms with your students. A great time to do this is at the start of the school year. Listen to your students and allow them to co-create their desired classroom culture. Ask them questions, guiding them to norms you want to include that they may not think of independently. Other helpful classroom norms could include active listening, respecting classmates, and being an ally and upstander, someone who supports and advocates for others. Once your students create their classroom norms, facilitate a discussion about what each norm looks like in action and what it doesn't.

For example, if promoting belonging is a classroom norm, ask your students what promoting belonging looks like in action and what it does not look like. When discussing what belonging doesn't look like, bring up microaggressions as an example, and do so in a school-appropriate and age-appropriate way. Explain what microaggressions are, how they can be unintentional but still cause harm, and their impact, and give examples of common microaggressions that students experience. Ask your students how they would feel if someone said something or behaved hurtfully toward them, even if it was unintentional. Also ask them how they would want to address and repair the harm done.

These questions are a natural segue into discussing how you expect your class to resolve conflict and have uncomfortable conversations. If a student intentionally or unintentionally does something hurtful to another student, how will you address it as a class? Together, create a plan that lets students have a voice in addressing and repairing the harm caused and create discussion norms and sentence stems for having these types of conversations.

Students may be uncomfortable discussing microaggressions when they occur. Help your students identify examples of what they can say or do if they experience or witness a microaggression. Teach your students to use simple phrases like, "What you said didn't feel right. It did not feel kind."

Teach your students to ask questions to unearth underlying assumptions. For instance, if a student hears their peer say something microaggressive to someone, or if an adult says something microaggressive toward them, teach students to ask questions such as, "Why do you think that?" or "Could you say more about what you mean by that?"

Also, come up with examples of how someone could acknowledge the hurt they caused, apologize, and take action to repair the harm. To repair the harm caused by a microaggression, the emotions and discomfort associated with it need to be acknowledged. For instance, your students can respond to a microaggressive comment by saying, "Let me tell you how that comment made me feel."

Give your students the space to repair the harm with the norms and language they create. Talking about microaggressions and how to address them will make students aware of them, less likely to commit them, and more comfortable bringing them up when they witness or experience them. Teach your students how to rely on restorative practices. You can use the book *Restorative Justice Tribunal and Ways to Derail Jim Crow Discipline* as a resource.

If you witness a microaggression and a student doesn't bring it up, address the microaggressive behavior with kindness and candor. Whether you or a student bring up the microaggressive behavior, use the moment to educate students about that particular microaggression and why it's harmful.

You may hear a student make a generalization about Black people based on stereotypes during a class discussion, for example. Blanket statements like "Black people are lazy, unintelligent, violent, criminals" or "Black people don't care about education" are harmful microaggressive stereotypes that need to be acknowledged and addressed immediately. Even seemingly innocuous statements are harmful, like "All Black people are good at sports" or "All Black people have rhythm."

If a student says or implies a blanket statement like those above, stop the class and point out why what the student said is untrue and harmful. You can further explain that when an entire race of people is reduced to one trait, the diversity within their human experience isn't recognized.

Explain why making blanket statements about Black people is harmful. People's limited views of African Americans impact how Black people move through the world and create barriers to success. If you overhear a comment like "You're the least scary Black guy I've ever met," for example, pause what your class is doing, deconstruct the belief that Black people are scary, and explain why that's untrue.

Another common microaggression is "I don't see color." People say that with good intentions, but that's received as "I don't see the beauty and richness in your ethnicity and culture, and I don't acknowledge that part of your identity."

When Black students' lived experiences are ignored, it fosters an unsafe and unwelcoming environment for them.

Whenever you hear microaggressions in your classroom, deconstruct the beliefs behind those statements and show why they're untrue and harmful. If your students don't have background knowledge or relationships with diverse people, they may not understand why microaggressions are hurtful. Cultivate a classroom culture where you intentionally encourage students to build relationships with each other. Facilitate classroom scavenger hunts where students have to find peers who have certain experiences or interests. Ask kids to get signatures from their classmates who have siblings, have visited a place outside of the United States, or play a musical instrument. Or play the beach ball icebreaker game where students toss a beach ball with "getting to know you" questions written on it: Their classmates get to pick which question on the beach ball to answer.

Students who have caring relationships with each other are more likely to discuss and learn from microaggressions when they occur. They will also be more likely to be mindful of microaggressions and not commit them.

Diverse Learning Materials Can Mitigate Biases that Are the Root of Race-Based Microaggressions

Many microaggressions stem from individuals' implicit biases. Exposing your students to different experiences and perspectives through diverse learning materials can help them see each other beyond any implicit biases or stereotypes they associate with others' identities.

Include books with diverse protagonists in your classroom library to expose students to diverse people. By featuring protagonists of different races, socioeconomic backgrounds, genders, and abilities, you'll give students opportunities to see reflections of themselves and their experiences and windows into the lives of people different from them.

Reflect on the learning resource materials you use. Consider the age-appropriate viewpoints of less commonly heard voices in the articles, videos, and resources you use in your lessons. When teaching about the history of voting rights, for example, discuss primary sources like Sojourner Truth's 1851 speech "Ain't I A Woman?" and Frances Ellen Watkins Harper's 1866 speech "We Are All Bound Together" (*Compare the Speeches – the Sojourner Truth Project*, n.d.) (BlackPast, 2011).

Incorporate ethnic names in math word problems (Jackson, 2022). In addition to using names like Bob, Ashley, and Clara, use names like Dewayne, Zamorah, Carlos, Gabriela, and Ibrahim. When doing so, be aware not to reinforce stereotypes of any group of people. Teachers sometimes, often unknowingly, bake stereotypes into math world problems (Nesher, 1980).

A teacher in Hillsboro, Oregon, found a math problem from an online resource that used migrant field workers and their level of productivity to help students learn about graph functions (Bright, 2020). The math problem portrayed migrant workers as incapable of being effective without supervision, focused on making profits rather than the exploitative conditions of migrant workers, and reinforced the stereotype that all Latinx people are lazy, foreigners, and field workers who work at low-wage jobs that nobody else wants. The teachers Black students need are mindful of the fact that math world problems often do not resemble problems in real-life situations. Find and create math word problems relevant to your students' lived experiences and that positively represent diverse people and their real-world experiences.

Using diverse materials can increase students' empathy and understanding of others and show them that there isn't only one way to experience and perceive the world. The students who these materials represent get to see their identities and experiences reflected back to them, and they can explore their own identities and relate their lived experiences to what they're learning.

> **Pause and Reflect**
>
> Do the materials you assign in your class act as windows and mirrors into the lives of your students? If not, what steps can you take to make the learning materials you assign more inclusive? Please share.
>
> _____
>
> _____
>
> _____

Address Race-Based Microaggressive School Policies

While many microaggressions are committed by individuals, some are built into school policies, like hair and dress codes. In 2018, a wrestling referee told Andrew Johson, a 16-year-old Black boy, that he had 90 seconds to decide between cutting his dreadlocks or forfeiting a wrestling match that would surely cost his team a division title (Washington, 2019).

The White referee, who had been previously suspended for calling a Black referee the N-word, told Andrew that he had to cut his hair because it was "unnatural." Andrew's hair was in regulation with The New Jersey State Interscholastic Athletic Association's hair rules. The referee committed a microassault; microassaults are explicit and derogatory. They're intentional discriminatory actions and verbal and nonverbal attacks like name-calling and avoidant behavior.

Under pressure, Andrew agreed to cut his dreads to continue competing with his team. He had tears in his eyes as his trainer chopped his dreadlocks. He won that match but struggled afterward. Other referees canceled his team's next two wrestling matches, citing that his hair was still illegal, more microaggressions.

Andrew struggled, wondering if the match cancellations were his fault. He struggled with everyone staring and whispering about him in his small town after a video of his dreadlocks being cut went viral. He struggled with comments that he should just get over it and that it's just hair. One night, he cut what was left of his dreadlocks with scissors from his kitchen. He loved his hair but was exhausted by being treated differently because of it.

Although Andrew wasn't violating the hair regulations, the regulations on hair length created room for discrimination. Andrew's experience isn't unique. There are dress codes across the nation that discriminate specifically against Black hair.

School officials threatened a 13-year-old boy in Texas with in-school suspension if he didn't allow school officials to color his fade haircut with black Sharpie, citing that his hair violated the school dress code (Fieldstadt, 2019). The Sharpie took days to wash off, and his peers bullied him; one called him a "thug," a microassault. He suffered from anxiety and depression afterward.

DeAndre Arnold, a high school senior, was suspended from school and forbidden from walking in his graduation ceremony unless he cut his dreadlocks. He transferred schools (Cox, 2020).

Seven-year-old Tiana Parker had a similar experience at her school in Oklahoma. Deborah Brown Community School gave Tiana an ultimatum to cut her dreadlocks or stop attending school (Persch, 2013). Their school policy stated that "hairstyles such as dreadlocks, afros, and other faddish styles are unacceptable."

Microaggressive policies and behaviors like these make Black students feel unwelcome at their schools and negatively impact their mental health and education. The teachers Black students need do all they can to help prevent experiences like these from happening to Black students at their schools.

Look at your school policies and dress codes to ensure they are free of biases that are harmful to your students of color. If there are biased policies at your school, bring them to your school administration or school board and suggest changes. Gathering the support of a group of teachers, staff, community members, parents, and guardians will help you when you approach your administration or school board.

3-2-1 Chapter Reflection

Take a moment to reflect on the content of the chapter and what it means to you.

What are three important ideas from this chapter?

_____
_____
_____

What are two action steps you can take based on this chapter?

_____
_____
_____

What is one concept you would like to explore in more depth?

_____
_____
_____

References

Allen, Q. (2010). Racial microaggressions: The schooling experiences of Black middle-class males in Arizona's secondary schools. *Journal of African American Males in Education*, 1(2), 125–143. https://digitalcommons.chapman.edu/cgi/viewcontent.cgi?article=1024&context=education_articles

Alsubaie, M. A. (2015). Hidden curriculum as one of current issue of curriculum. *Journal of Education and Practice*, 6(33), 125–128. https://files.eric.ed.gov/fulltext/EJ1083566.pdf

Andrews, R. S. (2023). *What Black students need from white teachers: A qualitative inquiry* [Theses and dissertations]. https://ir.library.illinoisstate.edu/cgi/viewcontent.cgi?article=2653&context=etd

Bean [Ahsante the Artist]. (2014, March 3). *I, too, am Harvard | Ahsante Bean | Ahsante the artist* [Video]. YouTube. www.youtube.com/watch?v=uAMTSPGZRiI

BlackPast, B. (2011, November 07). *(1866) Frances Ellen Watkins Harper, "We are all bound up together"*. BlackPast.org. www.blackpast.org/african-american-history/speeches-african-american-history/1866-frances-ellen-watkins-harper-we-are-all-bound-together/

Bright. (2020, June 5). *The problem with story problems*. Rethinking Schools. https://rethinkingschools.org/articles/the-problem-with-story-problems/

Civil Rights data collection: Data snapshot (school discipline). (2014, March 21). U.S. Department of Education Office for Civil Rights. https://civilrightsdata.ed.gov/assets/downloads/CRDC-School-Discipline-Snapshot.pdf

Compare the speeches. (2014). The Sojourner Truth Project. www.thesojournertruthproject.com/compare-the-speeches/

Cox, C. C. U. (2020, January 25). *Texas teen banned by high school from attending graduation after refusing to cut dreadlocks*. USATNetwork. https://eu.usatoday.com/story/news/nation/2020/01/24/black-texas-teen-barred-high-school-after-graduation-not-cutting-dreadlocks/4562210002/

Desautels, L. (2016, January 7). *Brains in pain cannot learn!* Edutopia. www.edutopia.org/blog/brains-in-pain-cannot-learn-lori-desautels

Fieldstadt, E. (2019, August 19). Parents sue after school employees colored in Black teen's haircut with marker [Video]. *NBC News*. www.nbcnews.com/news/us-news/texas-school-staffers-colored-black-teen-s-haircut-sharpie-lawsuit-n1043956

Gershenson, S., & Papageorge, N. (2017, October 24). The power of teacher expectations: How racial bias hinders student attainment. *Education Next*. www.educationnext.org/power-of-teacher-expectations-racial-bias-hinders-student-attainment/

The harmful effects of microaggressions. (n.d.). Today.duke.edu. https://today.duke.edu/2022/05/harmful-effects-microaggressions

Jackson, M. (2022). *Reconceptualizing mathematical word problems to reflect social justice principles and culturally relevant teaching* [Dissertation]. Nova Southeastern University.

Loewus, L. (2020, November 19). Research review: Teacher expectations matter. *Education Week*. www.edweek.org/leadership/research-review-teacher-expectations-matter/2013/01

Nesher, P. (1980). The stereotyped nature of school word problems. *For the Learning of Mathematics, 1*(1), 41–48. www.jstor.org/stable/40247701

Nieman, Y. F. (Producer). (2024, February 28). *Microaggressions in the classroom* [Youtube Video]. (Original work published 2017). https://docs.google.com/document/d/15uFxlblwx9VEBSuhSBHtfW0rYT3Ffj1y_JK6MTvxTg4/edit

Persch, J. (2013, September 10). *School that barred 7-year-old's dreadlocks changes dress-code policy*. TODAY.com. https://www.today.com/parents/school-barred-7-year-olds-dreadlocks-changes-dress-code-policy-8c11122821

Project Implicit. (2011). *Implicit association test*. Harvard.edu. https://implicit.harvard.edu/implicit/Study?tid=-1

Suttie, J. (2016, October 28). *Four ways teachers can reduce implicit bias*. Greater Good. https://greatergood.berkeley.edu/article/item/four_ways_teachers_can_reduce_implicit_bias

Terada, Y. (2022, April 21). *We drastically underestimate the importance of brain breaks*. Edutopia. www.edutopia.org/article/we-drastically-underestimate-importance-brain-breaks

Todd, R. (2021, October 27). *Recognizing the signs of trauma*. Edutopia. www.edutopia.org/article/recognizing-signs-trauma

Wamsted, J. (2021). *A simple way to self-monitor for bias.* www.edutopia.org/article/simple-way-self-monitor-bias/

Washington, J. (2019, September 18). The untold story of wrestler Andrew Johnson's dreadlocks. *Andscape.* https://andscape.com/features/the-untold-story-of-wrestler-andrew-johnsons-dreadlocks/

Willis, J. (2016, December 7). *Using brain breaks to restore students' focus.* Edutopia. www.edutopia.org/article/brain-breaks-restore-student-focus-judy-willis

Yeager, D. S., Purdie-Vaughns, V., Hooper, S. Y., & Cohen, G. L. (2017). Loss of institutional trust among racial and ethnic minority adolescents: A consequence of procedural injustice and a cause of life-span outcomes. *Child Development, 88*(2), 658–676. https://doi.org/10.1111/cdev.12697

4

Protect Black Students' Bodies From Harm

On a summer night in Las Vegas, a high school-aged student named Jamar found himself on his knees in an empty field with a pistol pressed against his head. Jamar had come alone to meet a person known as the "hook-up guy" to buy vintage sneakers at discount prices. He did not suspect he would wind up on his knees on the opposite side of a gun.

Jamar did his homework; he learned that the "Sneaker Man" did good business and did not sell stolen merch. That's why Jamar was there, to buy a mint-condition pair of the Air Jordan 11s trimmed in cherry red and white. When Jamar arrived where Sneaker Man said to meet him, Sneaker Man got out of the passenger side of a car with a shoe box under his left arm. The car driver got out, too, and fired up a blunt. Sneaker Man opened the shoebox and showed Jamar a pair of Jordan 11's in perfect condition.

"You got the $220?" Sneaker Man asked.

"Yeah. I got it," Jamar responded.

As Jamar reached for his wallet, the driver, blunt still in his mouth, punched Jamar in his jaw with a pair of brass knuckles. Jamar fell to the ground, feeling like his head had exploded. The ground was spinning. He struggled to get his balance and bearings and then felt cold metal pressed against his head.

The driver knew Jamar, but Jamar didn't know him. Earlier that summer, Jamar and one of his friends had burglarized a house. Jamar ran with a gang, but the burglary hadn't been gang business; it had been just for fun and sport. They stole a PlayStation, some money, and some jewelry. However, that house had been the driver's cousin's house, and the driver and his cousin belonged to a different gang that decided Jamar's disrespect could not go unpunished.

Jamar took a bullet to the head that night. He died instantly.

That murder kicked off a rash of neighborhood violence. Several fights and murders occurred throughout the community, and the beef and its tension spilled into my school. When these sorts of tensions spill into schools, it makes schools and classrooms feel unsafe to faculty, staff, students, and their families. It is urgently important to address these factors as they arise in order for schools to feel like safe spaces for all that are conducive to teaching and learning.

Schools Are Becoming More Violent

In September 2021, 22 students were arrested for fighting during a turbulent week at a high school in Louisiana (Karimi & Lemos, 2021). In February 2023, in Rochester, New York, a student attacked five staff members, picking up and slamming a security guard to the ground (Lewke, 2023). In November 2023, in Las Vegas, Nevada, teenagers attacked one of their schoolmates, 17-year-old Jonathan Lewis Jr., who died from his blunt force injuries six days later (Peguero & Romero, 2023).

Forty-six percent of public schools reported an increase in violence and fighting since the start of the COVID-19 pandemic, according to the National Center for Education Statistics' 2021–2022 survey (St. George, 2022). Over 80 percent of schools cited the toll the pandemic had on students' social and emotional development and behavior as the cause.

Gun violence has been on the rise since the pandemic, as well. When students returned to school after the pandemic, gun-related incidents increased by 170 percent (Wall, 2023). In the 2020–2021 school year, school shootings increased to the highest in two decades (Da Silva, 2022). Casualties increased, too: 44 people were killed and 149 people were wounded (*COE – Violent Deaths at School and Away From School, School Shootings, and Active Shooter Incidents*, n.d.). Those numbers increased the following school year: 71 people were killed and 206 people were wounded (Wolf, 2024). While the number of casualties decreased in the 2022–2023 school year, the number of school shootings increased (Wolf, 2024).

Feeling threatened and unsafe at work has prompted nearly half of teachers to consider quitting or transferring out of their schools (Grabmeler, 2022). Susan Dvorack McMahon, chairperson of the American Psychological Association Task Force on Violence Against Educators and School Personnel, asserts that harassment and violence against school staff is so formidable that it should be declared a public health crisis. This increase in aggressive behavior in schools is making students and staff feel unsafe ("Teachers, Other School Personnel, Experience Violence, Threats, Harassment During Pandemic," 2022).

Protect Black Students From Dangerous and Disruptive Schoolmates

Most students go to school every day to listen, learn, and enjoy their friends' company. Dangerous schoolmates should not interfere with any of these activities or cause Black students to fear for their safety. The teachers Black students need protect them from dangerous students and help students steer clear of dangerous situations.

Dangerous students are those who engage in violent or aggressive behavior that increases the likelihood of causing bodily injury to themselves or others. Students are dangerous when they bring weapons to school, fight repeatedly, and threaten school community members. The presence of dangerous students substantially disrupts teaching and learning in classrooms, as well as the normal functioning of school.

Increases in school violence have prompted lawmakers to make it easier for school personnel to remove dangerous or disruptive students from school, and a raft of legislation has passed (or is being considered) to achieve this goal (Wall, 2023). A bill in Florida passed that provides a "Teachers' Bill of Rights." Florida teachers have the right to control the classroom, which includes the right to remove disobedient students from their classrooms and use reasonable force to protect themselves and others from students who threaten others' safety (Solodev, n.d.). Florida teachers also have some safety from litigation for disciplining or removing students from their classroom written into the new law. It's presumed that they were taking "necessary action to restore or maintain the safety or educational atmosphere of his or her classroom" (Solodev, n.d.).

West Virginia passed a bill that lets teachers force "disorderly" students from their classrooms (Wall, 2023). Arizona and Nevada lawmakers passed legislation that allows students as young as kindergarteners to be suspended (*HB2460 – 561R – I Ver*, n.d.) (*Bill Tracking in Nevada – AB 194 (82 Legislative Session) – FastDemocracy*, n.d.). Kentucky lawmakers passed legislation that allows schools to permanently remove disruptive and dangerous students from their schools and place them in alternative settings (*Program > KET*, 2023).

Policies that exclude students from school disproportionately affect Black students the most (Pushed Out, 2022). When school discipline moves toward zero-tolerance policies, students of color and students who have disabilities are disproportionately suspended and expelled, miss more time out of class, and aren't given opportunities to learn new ways of communicating and resolving conflicts (Pushed Out, 2022). Because there is no learning opportunity, suspension and expulsion are not proven to be effective at *changing* dangerous and disruptive students' conduct, and out-of-school disciplinary responses should be issued as a last resort (Armstrong, 2018).

Therapeutic interventions and restorative practices are more effective for redirecting misbehaving students and keeping them in school. I go into great detail about this subject in the book *Restorative Justice Tribunal*. In that book, I explain how students, particularly Black students, get labeled as dangerous for benign behaviors that threaten nobody.

However, those aren't the students I'm referring to now: In this chapter, I'm referring to students who bring weapons to school, fight repeatedly, threaten school community members, commit crimes on campus, and perform other such behaviors. These are the students I am defining as dangerous and disruptive. These students should be removed from schools when they continuously violate behavior expectations and disrupt learning.

Check with your immediate supervisor or review your school handbook to learn the structures and processes to get help with dangerous or disruptive students in your school. Some schools expect teachers to use the intercom system to request assistance with dangerous or disruptive classroom situations. Other schools expect teachers to use their professional judgment to triage requests for help by submitting a behavior referral or for a teacher to handle the classroom disturbance on their own.

All students deserve to learn in a safe and respectful learning environment. While every student should have access to a high-quality education, some dangerous and disruptive students need a level of intervention that public schools are not designed to provide.

Use De-Escalation Techniques to Keep Your Classroom Community Orderly and Conducive to Learning

Teachers must know how their responses to student behavior can escalate or de-escalate students. De-escalation helps students reduce the intensity of problematic behavior quickly while keeping that student and others orderly and safe.

Some students have difficulty regulating their emotions. Students who are easily dysregulated may have trouble responding appropriately to situations or may react in explosive or aggressive ways. Emotional dysregulation is a symptom of mental health conditions like anxiety, oppositional defiant disorder, disruptive mood dysregulation disorder, and trauma-related disorders (*Emotional Dysregulation*, n.d.). It's also a symptom of neurodivergent experiences like ADHD and autism, as well as brain damage from strokes, substance abuse, and head injuries, for example.

Students who have difficulty regulating their emotions can be easily triggered when transitioning between classroom activities due to the lack of structure and uncertainty, for example, or when accidentally bumped by another student. When triggered, a student might start yelling or throw a chair because they don't know how to regulate their emotions.

When students are anxious and in a heightened emotional state, their cortisol levels increase. Cortisol is the stress hormone our glands release to help us respond rapidly in stressful situations. The release of cortisol impairs judgment, so it is important that we take steps to de-escalate students when they feel dysregulated, as well as help them recognize when they have heightened stress levels so they can de-escalate themselves.

Display open, accepting body language to disruptive students to reduce feelings of confrontation. Use simple, direct language when addressing students triggered by anxiety.

Keep your sentences brief and give students time to comprehend and to respond to what you say before continuing.

Give students time to calm themselves and help them plan what they will do the next time they feel anxious. Part of preventing disruptive behavior is teaching students to recognize their bodies' signs of anxiety and agitation and teaching them replacement behaviors that help them manage anxious moments as well as themselves.

Set aside an area of your classroom for de-escalation. It's best to have it in a quieter, less busy part of your classroom, which is why many teachers create calming corners, de-escalation stations in a corner of their classrooms. Make your de-escalation area an inviting and calming space. Bean bags, soft floor mats, plants, calming colors and photos, soft music, and noise-canceling earbuds are helpful for creating a calming and comfortable space. Include activities to help your students self-regulate as well. Fidget spinners, books, coloring pages, self-reflection writing prompts, and guided breathing exercises are helpful. If creating a de-escalation space in your classroom isn't physically possible, establish a habit of inviting students outside of your classroom to de-escalate.

When students act out aggressively or violently when they feel dysregulated, it's often not an intentional or malicious act to harm others. They don't have the skills to cope with their emotions, and often, their brains are wired in a way that makes it difficult to do so. Learning de-escalation strategies and teaching your students those strategies can help them self-regulate their emotions and behave appropriately in class.

You may experience students who need more support than you or your school can provide. In these situations, it may be best for your student to leave your class or school so they can get the support they need and so that the learning environment isn't disrupted for the rest of your students. Those are major decisions that are usually collaboratively by teams of educators, such as IEP teams, 504 teams, and administrative teams.

Know What's in Students' IEPs and 504 Plans to Ensure a Safe and Respectful Learning Environment

It's vital to know the behavioral goals of your students with disabilities and the content of their behavioral intervention plans. When special education professionals write behavioral goals and behavior intervention plans, they typically follow a functional behavioral assessment (FBA) process to determine where, when, and with whom targeted behaviors are the most and least likely to occur. As part of the FBA process, special education professionals identify behaviors and circumstances that precede the problematic behavior and identify replacement behaviors students need to learn to stay on track. They may also identify environmental and academic modifications that can help them.

Students' behavior intervention plans include goals and a roadmap to meet them; this helps students with special needs access the curriculum without being derailed by their behavior choices. Teaching social and emotional skills and alternative behaviors may be a part of your student's intervention plan. If they need more social-emotional support than you can provide, they may also meet with the school counselor individually or in a group. Your students may have environmental or academic modifications in their plans as well.

An environmental modification may be allowing a student to sit in a certain area in your classroom, or a place outside of the classroom like the library, so that they can have a distraction-free place to more easily focus on class work. An academic modification could be having the ability to take tests orally. Students' 504 plans function the same way. They communicate any behavioral supports a student may need.

It's important to know what's in your students' intervention plans so you can encourage positive behaviors and create learning environments that help your students get their needs met in a productive way that doesn't disrupt the learning or safety of others.

Monitor Students' Unstructured Time and Spaces

Students experience unstructured time when activities for them have not been structured, organized, or sequenced by an adult. There are no specific tasks for them to complete and there aren't clear behavioral expectations for how they should act. Recess, lunch times, and passing periods between classes are often unstructured or semi-structured at best. These are the times when students have more opportunities to misbehave or become disorderly. These are times when Black students can be exposed to physical harm by their peers or others.

It is important to monitor these unstructured activities in ways that prevent misbehavior before it starts. I know that teachers' daily schedules are demanding. You use the free time you have during lunch, recess, dismissal, and class changes to prep, grade, or ground yourself. When you use some of that time to invest in encouraging appropriate behavior outside of the classroom, you increase the likelihood of your students behaving appropriately in your class, and you increase the likelihood that your students won't replicate inappropriate behaviors they learn in unstructured spaces in your classroom

Stand outside your classroom door between classes. Walk through the lunchroom and greet students to provide extra supervision during lunch. Tell students how you expect them to behave during recess, while they eat their lunch, and while they are gathered before school in the morning. Appropriate behaviors during unstructured spaces and times should be taught and practiced. Don't assume that because students have been in school for a number of years they know how to behave during these times and in these spaces.

Invest the time to teach students how you expect them to behave during these times and in these spaces. Teach students how you expect them to walk in halls. Teach students how you expect them to behave while they wait for school to begin. Teach students how you expect them to behave in the lunchroom, particularly when they finish eating their food. Teach students how you expect them to behave during recess and what to do when they see their peers engage in risky or inappropriate behavior. Teach students how you expect them to behave as passengers on school buses.

The teachers Black students need understand that not only should they teach students how to behave in these unstructured spaces and during these unstructured times but also that behavior expectations in unstructured spaces may need to be retaught and repeatedly demonstrated to their students and that their students may need to practice them.

Pause and Reflect

When do your students have unstructured time in your classroom or school? How are students monitored during this time to ensure they behave kindly to each other? Please share.

_____

_____

_____

3–2–1 Chapter Reflection

Take a moment to reflect on the content of the chapter and what it means to you.

What are three important ideas from this chapter?

_____

_____

_____

What are two action steps you can take based on this chapter?

_____

_____

_____

What is one concept you would like to explore in more depth?

_____

_____

_____

References

Armstrong, D. (2018, April 4). Why suspending or expelling students often does more harm than good. *The Conversation*. https://theconversation.com/why-suspending-or-expelling-students-often-does-more-harm-than-good-93279

Bill tracking in Nevada – AB 194 (82 legislative session). (n.d.). *FastDemocracy*. https://fastdemocracy.com/bill-search/nv/82/bills/NVB00005908/

Da Silva, C. (2022, June 28). FBI data shows dramatic rise in school shootings in U.S. [Video]. *NBC News*. www.nbcnews.com/news/us-news/school-shootings-rose-highest-number-2-decades-federal-report-shows-rcna35638

Emotional dysregulation. (n.d.). Cleveland Clinic. https://my.clevelandclinic.org/health/symptoms/25065-emotional-dysregulation

Grabmeler, J. (2022, March 22). *Violence, threats have many teachers thinking about quitting*. College of Education and Human Ecology. https://ehe.osu.edu/news/listing/violence-threats-have-many-teachers-thinking-about-quitting

HB2460–561R – I Ver. (n.d.). www.azleg.gov/legtext/56leg/1r/bills/hb2460p.htm

Karimi, F., & Lemos, G. (2021, October 29). *Fights erupted at a high school in Louisiana. So these dads took matters in their own hands.* CNN. www.cnn.com/2021/10/29/us/dads-on-duty-louisiana-school-cec/index.html

Lewke, J. (2023, February 16). *Video shows student at school of the arts attacking staff members.* WHEC.com. www.whec.com/local/rpd-student-at-school-of-the-arts-attacked-staff-members-on-tuesday/

National Center for Education Statistics. (2023). Violent deaths at school and away from school, school shootings, and active shooter incidents. *Condition of Education.* U.S. Department of Education, Institute of Education Sciences. https://nces.ed.gov/programs/coe/indicator/a01

Peguero, J., & Romero, J. (2023, November 15). KRON4. www.kron4.com/news/national/las-vegas-teen-dies-after-group-attacks-him-near-high-school-father-says/

Program> KET. (2023, August 4). KET. https://ket.org/program/kentucky-tonight/student-discipline-legislation/

Pushed out: Trends and disparities in out-of-school suspension. (2022, September 30). Learning Policy Institute. https://learningpolicyinstitute.org/product/crdc-school-suspension-report

Solodev. (n.d.). *Teachers' bill of rights.* www.fldoe.org. www.fldoe.org/teaching/just-for-teachers-community/bill-of-rights.stml

St.George, D. (2022, July 6). Behavioral issues, absenteeism at schools increase, federal data shows. *Washington Post.* www.washingtonpost.com/education/2022/07/05/absenteeism-behavioral-issues-pandemic-data/

Teachers, other school personnel, experience violence, threats, harassment during pandemic. (2022, March 17). www.apa.org. www.apa.org/news/press/releases/2022/03/school-staff-violence-pandemic

Wall, P. (2023, November 9). With more shootings and guns on campus, schools walk a fine line in response. *Chalkbeat*. www.chalkbeat.org/2023/4/5/23670535/shootings-guns-schools-violence-metal-detectors-police/

Wolf, C. (2024, January 5). School shootings by state. *US News & World Report*. www.usnews.com/news/best-states/articles/states-with-the-most-school-shootings

5

Don't Let Grades Become Weapons Against Black Students

Children, I am concerned about the stress and anxiety that grades sometimes cause.

Grades can hurt. Grades are judgments, and how someone judges you impacts your feelings. I don't know that teachers always understand how their opinions affect you, including their opinions about your academic work.

I know you value your teachers and put great stock in how they feel about you. You were raised by teachers and were taught to respect your elders, and that increases the likelihood that you will take your teachers' judgments of you to heart.

I don't want grades to negatively affect your self-esteem. Know that you are much more than your grades and that your grades don't define who you are as a person, and understand that every teacher's judgment of you won't be fair.

You must be a critical consumer of schooling. Go into your classrooms with your eyes open. Just as nurses and medical providers need a bedside manner while caring for patients, teachers must have a "deskside manner" while teaching students.

DOI: 10.4324/9781003529507-5

All your teachers won't have a pleasant deskside manner, so I want you to know what a poor deskside manner looks and feels like so you can advocate for yourself and ask for support when you're being treated unfairly. I want you to tell your mom or me about any uncomfortable conversations you have with your teachers about your schoolwork or otherwise.

Don't get me wrong. I expect your teachers to give you appropriate, even tough, corrective feedback when needed. Making mistakes and receiving corrective feedback is an important part of learning. But please understand I don't expect teachers to be mean to you, belittle you, or make you feel bad about yourself when they give you grades or feedback. Feedback absent of care and instructional direction is destructive.

The Case of Reva and Brook Stevens

In Meadowville High School, there were two students named Reva and Brook Stevens. They were honor students taking dual-enrollment courses, college classes available to high school students. The Stevens sisters earned exceptional grades in all their classes, and their conduct was exemplary. By all accounts, Reva and Brook were wonderful young ladies.

Reva and Brook were also religious. Their faith played a major role in their lives. They prayed in front of the flagpole every day before school and attended church several times a week. Occasionally, they had missionary duties during the day that caused them to miss school. They brought an absence excuse note signed by their mother and church minister every time they were absent.

The excused absences did not sit well with Ms. Sabrina Cliff, their dual enrollment English teacher. Ms. Cliff wanted to fail the Stevens sisters. She told Reva and Brook that she would transfer them out of her class because they missed too many group assignments to pass the course. The girls were devastated, and their devastation turned to anger.

Reva and Brook complained to their school counselor, Ms. Kennedy, who advocated on their behalf to the principal. She told their principal that Reva and Brook had no unexcused absences all school year and numerical averages of over 90 percent in Ms. Cliff's class. As a result, the principal sent Ms. Cliff a memo directing her to honor the Stevens sisters' excused absences and to create alternatives to in-class assignments for students with excused absences.

Be Aware of Academic Grading Bias

Teachers are human. We make mistakes. Like Ms. Cliff, teachers have feelings, and biases, and can behave hurtfully, sometimes unknowingly. Some of that hurtful behavior includes or affects grading. Fair, accurate grading is important because students, parents, college admissions, and employers see grades as a reflection of a student's capability. Students' grades impact their future.

The teachers Black students need are mindful of their biases and how their biases impact their professional practice, including how they assign grades. Biases are anchored in beliefs about race, gender, sexual orientation, or other criteria, and unfortunately, grading bias disproportionately affects Black students negatively (Tyner, 2020). Teachers unaware of their biases sometimes give grades based on criteria unrelated to students' mastery of learning targets or academic standards. There is a body of research that supports this unfortunate reality for Black students.

In one study, educators were asked to grade papers of anonymous, fictitious second-grade students (Quinn, 2020). The assignments were identical in every way, except a sibling's name, Connor or Deshawn. Researchers found that White women teachers – 79 percent of the US teacher workforce – who graded the work of "Deshawn's" brother were significantly less likely to grade the assignment as "on grade level" (Will, 2020) Teachers of color and male teachers did not exhibit the same bias. Conversely, when teachers were asked to grade the same assignment based on a scoring rubric, study participants exhibited no bias.

To reduce grading bias, use rubrics and anonymous grading when you can. Have students write their names on the last page of papers, exams, and quizzes. Also, some learning management systems like Canvas and Blackboard have anonymous grading options. It might be prudent to use them to prevent academic grading bias.

Be Aware of Behavioral Grading Bias

Grading biases impact not only academic grades but also citizenship grades. Research shows that African-American students often receive lower citizenship grades than their White peers, especially in classrooms taught by White teachers (Tyner, 2020). The root of this phenomenon lies in the implicit biases that affect teachers' assessments of what Black students know and are capable of achieving.

To assess how your own implicit biases might be affecting your citizenship grades, use the same tracking exercise you did in the chapter "Don't Let Microaggressions Define Black Students' Classroom Experiences." Track your interactions with your students for a month with a clipboard (Wamsted, 2021). Track which students you discipline, whose raised hands you call on, who you cold call, and which students you joke with and ask about their interests outside of the classroom.

If you discover that you interact with your Black students inequitably compared with your other students, you have a starting point to work on. You now have a list of students who you can make a point to have conversations with, call on when they raise their hands, question whether you need to discipline them so severely or at all, and question whether you're giving them fair citizenship and academic grades when reviewing their behavior and work.

Equity in grading matters. Equitable grading practices lead to better student-teacher relationships, reduced failure rates, less stressful classrooms, and grades more correlated to the level of students' mastery of standards (Feldman, 2020a).

Ensure Grades Reflect What Students Know and Can Do

Grades should reflect students' progress toward mastering standards. Grades should not be based on superfluous criteria, as Ms. Cliff attempted with the Stevens sisters. Ms. Cliff used grades to force her students to comply with expectations unrelated to learning targets and academic standards. She used grades to enforce her attendance expectations, which did not align with her school's policies.

Because grades communicate students' understanding, they should be used as a teaching tool, not punitive discipline, which disproportionately affects Black students (Winterman, 2021). Attendance, behavior, or forgetting to write a name on an assignment shouldn't affect students' grades. Similarly, students' grades shouldn't be inflated. Sometimes teachers worry about how many Ds or Fs they give students on their report cards, particularly when their schools monitor D and F rates. Still, inflating students' grades does no favors for students and contributes to achievement gaps.

Give Students Helpful, High-Quality Feedback

Feedback should be one step in a learning process that provides students direction to improve their academic performance, not a culminating activity or final step. Feedback on grades and formative assessments is a teaching tool. Because it's a teaching tool, it's important to use grading rubrics that clearly outline your expectations and grading criteria for each assignment so that students know what they need to do to achieve mastery.

How you give feedback to students is important, too. To ensure your students hear your feedback and find it helpful, give corrective feedback that is objective, timely, specific, supportive, and actionable (*Corrective Feedback | WingInstitute.org*, n.d.). Ensure your feedback points to specific examples of what a student did well and what they need to work on in relation to your grading rubric, and then provide specific suggestions on how they can improve their performance.

It's also important to praise specific behaviors in your feedback. Praise is powerful and positively impacts students' self-worth. Don't just write "great job" on assignments, leaving students wondering what was "great" about their work. Instead, highlight specific things that your students did well and why it was done well.

When you do that, you're building trust and communicating to your students that you believe they are capable of meeting your high expectations. Unfortunately, that's not a common experience for Black students. It's common for Black students to be made to feel less capable than their White peers and to be told by counselors and teachers to not set their expectations too high.

When you communicate your high expectations to students, their self-awareness and efficacy increase, they set higher goals, and they have better academic outcomes (Protective Factors, n.d.). It may seem overwhelming to change the feedback you give and the ways you give it, but Grant Wiggins outlines seven important features of effective feedback that you can focus on as a start.

Seven Keys to Effective Feedback

Adapted from Grant Wiggins via ASCD

1. **Goal-Referenced**: Your feedback should be given with the intent to help your student reach a goal. It can be helpful to specifically reference that goal in your feedback to remind both you and the student what the ideal result is.
2. **Tangible and Transparent**: If your student can't understand your feedback, they won't be able to apply or learn from it. They should also be able to determine what your desired result is and how they can best get there.
3. **Actionable**: Similarly, if your student doesn't know what to do with feedback, they won't be able to improve. Your feedback should provide clear steps that your student can take to reach their goal.
4. **User-Friendly**: Your student won't be able to learn from your feedback if it's too technical or too overwhelming. Focus on the most important things first and then elaborate or expand if your student clearly understands your feedback.
5. **Timely**: Feedback that arrives too late will not be as useful since your student could have moved on to a different goal or forgotten what specifically they're being evaluated on. Do your best to ensure you give feedback as soon as possible.
6. **Ongoing**: Your feedback should not be a "one and done" deal; your student should have opportunities to put it in practice and then receive more feedback. Otherwise, it can be hard to determine whether your student is getting closer to their goal.
7. **Consistent**: In order to improve and reach their goal, your student needs to be able to trust and rely on

their feedback. In addition to focusing on your own consistence, work with other teachers to make sure you're evaluating students similarly.

(Wiggins, 2012)

Make Your Classroom an Academically and Psychologically Safe Space

The majority of high-achieving students feel stressed about grades. A Stanford University study revealed that about 75 percent of high-achieving high school students felt stressed about their schoolwork and worried about taking tests and quizzes (Feldman, 2020b). That pressure to get good grades contributes to anxiety, poor sleep, and even self-harm for some students. That's why it's important to build classroom cultures where your students feel comfortable taking academic risks, including getting, giving, and making sense of feedback.

To create a safe classroom culture where giving and receiving feedback is the norm, it's important to establish relationships with your students defined by care, kindness, and psychological safety. Ensuring Black students can see themselves represented in the classroom and learning materials is one way to create academic and psychological safety in your classroom. Correctly pronouncing your Black students' names, incorporating their interests into assignments, and embracing the natural intersections between race and learning standards are other ways to create a classroom culture where your Black students feel safe to take academic risks.

In order to have an effective feedback culture, students also need to feel safe making mistakes publicly. Sharing your mistakes is a great way to show that mistakes are okay and that even teachers don't get everything right.

> **Pause and Reflect**
> How do you ensure your classroom is a place where mistakes are regarded as waypoints to learning? Please share.
>
> _____
>
> _____
>
> _____

However, normalizing failure as part of the learning process and effectively giving corrective feedback may not be enough when working with students who have experienced trauma. Trauma influences how students respond to corrective feedback. Students who have endured trauma may have extreme reactions to setbacks, disproportionate difficulty managing their emotions, and difficulty interacting with their peers, and they may be especially forgetful or unfocused (Todd, 2021). Teachers who do a poor job of giving effective feedback can trigger trauma that students bring with them to school. In fact, teachers can be the source of trauma for some students.

When students' fight, flight, or freeze response is triggered, the parts of the brain that control executive functioning skills like working memory, emotional regulation, active listening, problem-solving, and decision-making start to shut down (Flannery, 2016) (Brann, 2022). And if a student is triggered by feedback, they won't be able to hear it, receive it, and learn from it.

How The Teachers Black Students Need Assign Grades

The teachers Black students need understand that grades should communicate progress toward meeting learning targets and mastering academic standards and that assessment practices must positively impact learning. They evaluate students' learning using research- and standards-based grading practices that are fair, accurate, specific, and timely, and they use grading rubrics to make grading criteria clear and to avoid grading bias (Quinn, 2020).

Too many grading practices commonly used today have inequitable impacts on students, each with different implications. For instance, curving grades turn assessments into a competition and undermine student collaboration, and 0–100 grade scales disproportionately assign over half of the grading scale to a failing grade (an F) (Feldman, 2020b). Making homework or classwork a major part of a grade undermines the purpose of these assignments as practice, and participation grades assess behaviors rather than what a student knows (Feldman, 2020b).

Averaging grades over a longer time period doesn't accurately reflect where students are or how much they know at a given moment (Hough, 2023). And awarding or subtracting points based on class conduct, timeliness, or neatness allows teachers' implicit biases to influence grading and doesn't reflect students' mastery of learning targets. None of these grading practices allows students space to improve upon mistakes, which is counterproductive to how students learn (Feldman, 2019).

> **Pause and Reflect**
>
> Are the assessment practices you use equitable for all students? What changes can you make, if any, to make your assessment practices more equitable? Please share.
>
> _____
> _____
> _____

3–2–1 Chapter Reflection

Take a moment to reflect on the content of the chapter and what it means to you.

What are three important ideas from this chapter?

_____
_____
_____

What are two action steps you can take based on this chapter?

_____
_____
_____

What is one concept you would like to explore in more depth?

_____
_____
_____

References

Brann, A. (2022, January 22). Stress and memory. *Synaptic Potential.* https://synapticpotential.com/emotion/stress-and-memory/

Corrective feedback. (n.d.). www.winginstitute.org. www.winginstitute.org/instructional-delivery-feedback

Feldman, J. (2019, April 29). Beyond standards-based grading: Why equity must be part of grading reform. *Kappan Online.* https://kappanonline.org/standards-based-grading-equity-reform-feldman/

Feldman, J. (2020a, February 3). *Accurate and equitable grading.* www.nsba.org/ASBJ/2020/February/Accurate-Equitable-Grading

Feldman, J. (2020b, September 1). *Taking the stress out of grading.* ASCD. www.ascd.org/el/articles/taking-the-stress-out-of-grading

Flannery, M. E. (2016, May 17). *How trauma is changing children's brains*. NEA. www.nea.org/nea-today/all-news-articles/how-trauma-changing-childrens-brains

Hough, L. (2023, May 19). *The problem with grading*. Harvard Graduate School of Education. www.gse.harvard.edu/ideas/ed-magazine/23/05/problem-grading

Protective Factors. (n.d.). *National Center of safe supportive learning environments*. U.S. Department of Education. https://safesupportivelearning.ed.gov/training-technical-assistance/education-level/early-learning/protective-factors

Quinn, D. M. (2020, November 2). How to reduce racial bias in grading. *Education Next*. www.educationnext.org/how-to-reduce-racial-bias-in-grading-research/

Todd, R. (2021, October 27). *Recognizing the signs of trauma*. Edutopia. www.edutopia.org/article/recognizing-signs-trauma

Tyner, A. (2020). *Reducing grading bias against Black students*. The Thomas B. Fordham Institute. https://fordhaminstitute.org/national/commentary/reducing-grading-bias-against-black-students

Wamsted, J. (2021, January 22). *A simple way to self-monitor for bias*. Edutopia. www.edutopia.org/article/simple-way-self-monitor-bias/

Wiggins, G. (2012, September 1). *Seven keys to effective feedback*. ASCD. https://ascd.org/el/articles/seven-keys-to-effective-feedback

Will, M. (2020, November 19). Still mostly white and female: New federal data on the teaching profession. *Education Week*. www.edweek.org/leadership/still-mostly-white-and-female-new-federal-data-on-the-teaching-profession/2020/04

Winterman, L. (2021, October 7). *For Black students, unfairly harsh discipline can lead to lower grades*. www.apa.org. www.apa.org/news/press/releases/2021/10/black-students-harsh-discipline

6

Use Your Voice to Advocate for Black Students

Zahra, Zaire, and Zamorah, do you remember when I ran for North Las Vegas City Council? Zahra, you asked me what a city council election was and why I was running. I explained that the city council makes decisions that impact us, our neighbors, and the school district and how the city councilor representing us and our neighborhood seemed unaware of our needs.

He didn't talk with people in our neighborhood or teachers to learn about the challenges neighborhood children faced daily. He didn't know what teachers needed to reach children better. I was sure he was well-intentioned, but he was absent.

When I ran for city council, I went to community forums, rang doorbells, and put out signs – all the things candidates do. I also made a point to talk to voters about our schools, the hard work of teachers, and students' needs.

I lost the election. However, I learned lessons about myself and about running for public office. I learned that I cared deeply about North Las Vegas, especially the citizens who, for whatever reason, were disengaged from political processes. I also learned that

DOI: 10.4324/9781003529507-6

municipal elections are key to improving the lives of everyday people, and school board elections and the policies school board members set directly influence the education Black children receive. If teachers want to influence policies and conditions that impact teaching and learning, they have to engage with their elected school boards, parent advocates, and other elected officials. Getting involved in school board elections and dialoguing with families and other elected officials is a powerful and effective way for teachers to become the advocates Black students need.

Your Voice Is a Powerful Tool

You are an education professional trained to diagnose and respond to students' academic needs. Politicians, interest groups, and parents de-professionalize the teaching profession when they disregard your expertise. Too many career educators aren't given the space and autonomy to do what they were trained to do, making it more difficult for teachers to teach in ways that lead to positive student outcomes.

It can feel disempowering when you teach in a place that limits what you can teach and how you can support your students. It's common to feel defeated and frustrated when parents condemn your teaching practices, your school board doesn't support what you do, and politicians make choices that don't benefit your students. When it feels like everything and everyone is against you, advocating for yourself and your students can seem hopeless.

Other teachers across the country are experiencing this with you; you're not alone, and there are ways to assert your expertise. The most powerful tool you have to advocate for what you and your students need is your voice. You know your students, and you know their educational needs. Great education experiences absolutely can result from a collaboration between educators and non-educators. That being said, politicians, interest groups, and parents don't have your experience or the understanding of your students in your classroom. They don't understand pedagogy like you do.

Some parents, special interest groups, and politicians in some places are rallying to take away your agency as a teacher. By understanding how these groups work, their impact, and how you can leverage your voice, you'll be better equipped to strengthen your agency and advocate for what's best for your students.

Parents, Special Interest Groups, and Politicians Are Influencing What Teachers Teach

Parents, special interest groups, and politicians understand the impact that setting policy has on dictating what is taught in your classroom, and they understand the impact that being vocal has on swaying public opinion. They are influencing federal, state, local, and district policies across the country, determining the education your students can and cannot receive.

An eighth-grade history teacher in Iowa chose not to renew his contract last year after speaking to his superintendent and a school board member about whether he could teach that "Slavery was wrong" under House File 802, an Iowa law that "prohibits the use of curriculum that teaches the topics of sexism, slavery, racial oppression, racial segregation, or racial discrimination" (Iowa Legislative Services Agency, 2023) (Harris, 2023) (Reynolds, 2021).

His superintendent couldn't give him a clear answer. The school board member told him to teach both sides of slavery and gave the Holocaust as an example: Instead of stating that the Holocaust was wrong, he was told to teach that some people believed the Holocaust was wrong and some people believed it right.

According to researchers at the University of California, Los Angeles (UCLA), as of 2023, 49 states have made efforts to ban Critical Race Theory (CRT) from being taught in K-12 education, higher ed, and government agencies (Alexander et al., n.d.). Ninety-four percent of all local and state government attempts to ban teaching CRT are focused on K-12 education. To comply with these laws, almost 25 percent of US English, math, and science teachers from a national sample of 8,000 educators eliminated or limited discussions of race and gender from their instructional materials (Owens, 2023).

Florida, one of the states focused on anti-CRT legislation, passed a law that prohibits educators from teaching about race in a way that would make their students "feel discomfort, guilt, anguish, or any other form of psychological distress" about their race due to historical events (*House Bill 7 (2022) – the Florida Senate*, n.d.). This law – just like laws throughout other states and school districts – is meant to protect White and non-Black students from potential emotional discomfort. These policies come from a place of anxiety. They come from a place of fear that the content will be taught with a political slant at the expense of teaching history truthfully, fairly, and in a balanced way.

Admittedly, some teachers make the poor choice of infusing their political views into their teaching of content standards. However, this is not the norm. Most teachers adhere to their duty to teach standards in unbiased ways that allow students to form their own opinions. Teachers are education professionals, and ongoing training can help teachers to teach subjects unbiasedly.

Some parents advocate for these new policies inhibiting teachers' instructional freedom. They understand the power of their voices and have formed political action committees (PACs) and special interest groups to influence education policies at the federal, state, and district levels, even putting millions of dollars into local board elections to influence their outcomes and policies (Binkley & Smyth, 2022).

Special interest groups and PACs are groups formed to pursue common interests and influence decisions on public matters, including aligning educational content with particular political philosophies. The parental rights movement has created a surge of PACs and special interest groups seeking to modify how and what teachers teach in at least 34 of 50 states throughout America.

In 2022, 85 bills in 26 states were pre-filed or introduced to expand parents' rights in schools (DiMarco, 2022). As of the writing of this book, six have been enacted as law: two in Florida, two in Arizona, and one each in Georgia and Louisiana. With expanded parental rights, school districts and states across the country are banning discussions about race, sexual orientation, and gender identity from school materials and curricula.

These laws may be impacting you.

> **Pause and Reflect**
> To what degree is your classroom a safe space for students to discuss race and ethnicity? Please share.
> _____
> _____
> _____

Understanding What Rights Parents Do and Don't Have in Your Classroom

It's important to know what parents have the right to do and what they don't have the right to do so that you can advocate, and quite frankly collaborate, for the best education for all of your students.

Parents have the right to opt their kids out of class instruction that they disagree with philosophically, such as sex education. It is okay that parents ask educators to refrain from "indoctrinating" students with political views. Children should feel free to form their own opinions. Just as you had opportunities to come to your own conclusions on issues and wonderings, students deserve opportunities to do the same.

However, parents should not be entitled to censor standards-based, age-appropriate, and accurate instruction solely because it makes them uncomfortable. They should not be able to dictate teachers' unbiased, professional presentation of age-appropriate, standards-based content. Allowing students to discuss race as it relates to curriculum content isn't political, but censoring age-appropriate, standards-based discussions about realities that affect them is. Students will have fewer opportunities to form their own ideas about the world if interest groups, parents, or policymakers successfully sanitize school curricula.

> **Pause and Reflect**
> Have you ever felt uncomfortable discussing a topic in your class even though the topic was related to a state-approved academic standard? Please share.
> _____
> _____
> _____

Every child and their family has a right to public schooling, but schooling will not meet every family's needs. Families have every right to homeschool or enroll their children in private school if they don't want their children to discuss current events that impact them or if public schools don't share their family's beliefs. That's fair and fine.

Public schools, by their design, prepare students to coexist with diverse groups of people and explore a diversity of ideas. Black children and their peers should be free to experience age-appropriate, standards-based, objective discussions that will help them navigate their worlds, but some parental rights groups and politicians are working hard, sometimes unknowingly, to censor these discussions.

Parents and community members can and should be involved in their children's education. It is not unreasonable for families to want to ensure that students are not exposed to age-inappropriate or politically biased presentation of curriculum content. By developing relationships with parents, you can help them understand why you teach certain content standards the way you do and why certain class conversations are necessary to help students master curriculum standards. While some parents will remain firm in their belief that any discussion about race is political and not welcome in the classroom, others are simply misinformed, and talking with them can resolve any issues.

If you receive outside pressure from parents trying to restrict your ability to teach standards-based content related to race, it can be overwhelming. While there aren't silver bullet solutions for dealing with that kind of stress, you can take actions to navigate parent opposition. When parents want to see changes at their school, they go to the school board to advocate for what they believe is best for their kids. That is their right, and it is your right, too.

Collaborate With Your Superintendent

As a teacher, your voice matters. It may sometimes seem like it doesn't. You may not be in a supportive work environment in your district or because of your city, county, or state policies. But you have a unique perspective that outside influences don't have: you know your students and their needs. If your superintendent advocates for accessible and equitable academic outcomes for all students, there are things you can do to support your superintendent's work.

The teachers Black students need are conscious of how their superintendent is supervised by their school board. School boards have one employee, the superintendent. A superintendent may support your efforts to create safe and respectful classrooms where Black students thrive, and your school board can, sometimes unknowingly, block such efforts. School boards sometimes fire superintendents for advocating for equity.

A school board in Oregon banned teachers from displaying symbols in support of LGBTQIA+ Pride and Black Lives Matter and fired the superintendent because of it (KTAR, 2021). In a school district in South Carolina, two hours after six conservative school board members were sworn in, they fired the superintendent, banned critical race theory, and established a committee to decide which books should be banned in the school district (Kingkade, 2022). In Colorado, a school board terminated a superintendent after he insisted the school district follow its equity policy (Brundin, 2022). In Oklahoma, a school board fired a school district superintendent for speaking out against a letter written by the Oklahoma Secretary of Education that asked textbook publishers to reconsider any content that may contain critical race theory (Moss/KFOR, 2022).

It is hard to be a teacher Black students need when your superintendent meets resistance when they give you agency to develop diverse students' talents. Ironically, doing what's right for children can be extremely isolating for superintendents. Sometimes, the 'right thing' to do is not the popular, safe choice and has uncomfortable professional repercussions. Supporting your superintendent goes a long way in forwarding an agenda of high-quality education and equitable educational outcomes for all students. Here are some ways to support superintendents focusing on equitable student outcomes.

1. Let them know that you appreciate the work they do. Write your superintendent a letter. Tell them what

you're grateful for regarding their leadership and what they do for you and your students.

A heartfelt and supportive letter goes a long way. When the path to ensuring schooling meets all children's needs becomes politically prickly and perilous and when workdays get especially long, I have a folder of letters from teachers and community members that I read. Those letters keep me grounded and assure me that I'm making decisions in the best interest of students.

It's also helpful to write letters to your state legislators about how the legislation they discuss will impact you and your students. If your state legislators are undecided on a bill, receiving an outpouring of letters can sway their decision. That can help create a more conducive environment for your superintendent to support you in meeting your students' needs.

2. Share your experiences with the school board on matters directly affecting you and your students. Explain how what they are voting on will positively or negatively impact your students and clarify any misunderstandings they may have.

Sharing your opinion publicly can be intimidating, whether in person or over Zoom. If speaking publicly isn't your thing, you can share your voice in other ways. Email your board members written testimonies about board meeting agenda items.

Write an anonymous letter to your school board members. Sometimes, speaking publicly might not be safe, especially when discussing a divisive topic. If that's the case for you, you can send an anonymous letter.

Encourage other teachers and community members to tell school boards their perspectives on diversity, equity, and inclusion concerns when they surface, whatever their opinion is. The dialogue is instructive and an important aspect of civic engagement.

Most school board members welcome your feedback on policies and procedures. Your school board does not make decisions in a vacuum. School board members are community members who care deeply about schools, but few tend to have a background in education. School board members rely on community opinions to inform their decisions. They don't work with students day in and day out. You do. You have expertise, experience, and a perspective that's valuable and necessary for them to hear.

3. Join a policy committee and help shape school district policies. As a superintendent, if the school board was going to discuss an action or policy that may be divisive, I'd send it to the policy committee for discussion and, ultimately, recommendations for the board. The policy committee was made up of a diverse group of students, teachers, school staff, and community members. They vetted potential policies, procedures, and actions before the board votes on them to ensure they are aligned with the community's beliefs and are in the best interest of all students.

When you have a superintendent who supports your vision for equity, these actions can go a long way in getting the agency and resources you need to support your students.

Encourage Students to Be Informed Voters

Voter turnout for any election – presidential to local – is the lowest among 18- to 29-year-olds (*Voter turnout*, 2023). These are your students. These are your students who stop you at the grocery store or a restaurant and share with you the impact you had on their lives. These are your students whose children you now teach. They have the power to vote in federal, state, and local school board elections, impacting the resources and instructional freedom or limitations you'll have and the quality of education that future generations will receive, including their children.

It's easy to think that young adults don't vote because they don't care about politics or are disillusioned by it, and some may be. But according to political science researchers and authors of the 2020 book *Making Young Voters: Converting Civic Attitudes into Civic Action*, young adults' interest in politics and voting is high, but there are various barriers in place preventing them from voting: policy barriers, transiency, not feeling informed enough to vote, a lack of knowledge about how to register, and a lack of executive functioning skills to follow through on their desire to vote (Hillygus, 2020).

All of these barriers can be weakened through education. It's never too early to teach about civic engagement. Explain to your students the power of their vote and encourage them to vote when they turn 18. The act of voting is not a partisan issue. There's nothing wrong with teaching students that voting is an important form of civic engagement, but engaging in political proselytizing is not okay. Teachers that Black children need prepare students to be informed citizens who participate in the democratic process.

Teach your students how voting works and the process they must go through to cast their votes. Discuss the voting laws and restrictions in the state you teach in. Some states have laws and limitations that make it more difficult for recent 18-year-olds to vote. Make sure your high school students are aware of these laws and know the processes they'll have to go through to be able to vote in their first election once they turn 18.

Walk your students through different voting scenarios. You can start by showing students how to register to vote;

not knowing how to register is one reason young people don't vote. Walk your students through requesting a mail-in ballot or registering to vote in another state. Many young adults don't vote when they go to college out of state because they don't know how to. Youth encouraged to vote or taught how to register are more likely to vote and engage in civic activities.

Simulate the power of the vote by allowing students to vote on some classroom or whole-school policies. Ask your local voting commission or secretary of state to facilitate mock elections in your school. Find out if voting booths can be brought into your school so students can experience what it is like to vote in an election. Teach your students the importance of voting for local and school board elections and the impact that school boards have on their education.

Teach your students how elections work and the history of voting. In addition to equipping students with the skills to vote, educate your students about campaigning, the Electoral College, and the history of the fight for suffrage in America. Let students investigate why groups of people throughout American history fought for voting rights.

Teach your students about the impact of redistricting. On its face, redistricting is nothing more than an effort for municipalities to comply with apportionment laws and ensure voting districts keep up with population changes. Unfortunately, redistricting can also create inequities and diminish the voices of groups of people when it's manipulated to pack voters with a political perspective into one district or to spread voters likely to support a particular political view across many districts, diluting their voting power (Maddock, 2020). This is when redistricting devolves into gerrymandering.

Teach your students about the history and impact of gerrymandering. Historically, gerrymandering primarily and negatively impacted communities of color and low-income communities, contributing to low-income students and students of color being confined to underperforming, underfunded schools. As an example, in 2011, after Americus, Georgia, was redistricted, they went from a majority to a minority African-American school board, no longer representing their majority African-American student population (Casey, 2021). Improving Black children's education no longer seemed to be a priority of the new school board.

Teach your students to pay attention to redistricting and how the process works in your district or region. Educate them on any proposed boundary changes and the potential impact on the distribution of resources, racial composition, and the socioeconomic composition of schools. Show students how they can write letters and make phone calls to their elected officials to express their concerns about the impact of redistricting on them and their school. Call your elected official in class so they can see you go through the process yourself.

Young people are highly interested in politics but don't know how to vote or feel ill prepared to do so. When you give your students the tools to be civically engaged, you're teaching them that their voices matter and that they have the power to shape their communities. Many of them will become adults in the community you teach in.

Pause and Reflect

Have you ever shared your perspectives with decision-makers in your school or district? If so, how did you do that? Please share.

_____

_____

_____

_____

3–2–1 Chapter Reflection

Take a moment to reflect on the content of the chapter and what it means to you.

What are three important ideas from this chapter?

_____
_____
_____

What are two action steps you can take based on this chapter?

_____
_____
_____

What is one concept you would like to explore in more depth?

_____
_____
_____

References

Alexander, T., Clark, L., Reinhard, K., & Zatz, N. (n.d.). *CRT firward* [Review of CRT Forward]. Retrieved April 30, 2024, from https://crtforward.law.ucla.edu/wp-content/uploads/2023/04/UCLA-Law_CRT-Report_Final.pdf

Binkley, C., & Smyth, J. C. (2022, October 11). Conservative PACs inject millions into local school races. *AP News.* https://apnews.com/article/entertainment-elections-education-school-boards-teaching-059f2465829ab009394469b-95c8cc94a

Brundin, J. (2022, April 14). *Former DougCo superintendent says he was fired illegally over support for masking, equity policies.* Colorado Public Radio. www.cpr.org/2022/04/14/douglas-county-corey-wise-termination-complaint/

Casey, N. (2021, October 10). A voting rights battle in a school board 'Coup'. *The New York Times*. www.nytimes.com/2020/10/25/us/politics/voting-rights-georgia.html

DiMarco, B. (2022, June 6). Legislative tracker: 2022 parent-rights bills in the states. *FutureEd*. www.future-ed.org/legislative-tracker-parent-rights-bills-in-the-states/

Harris, M. (2023, April 24). The Iowa social studies teacher who quit because he couldn't tell his students that slavery was wrong. *Slate Magazine*. https://slate.com/news-and-politics/2023/04/iowa-critical-race-theory-curriculum-slavery-holocaust-teacher-quit.html

Hillygus, S. (2020, October 20). *The missing youth vote*. Issues in Science and Technology. https://issues.org/real-reason-young-people-dont-vote-hillygus/

House bill 7 (2022) – the Florida Senate. (2022). Flsenate.gov. www.flsenate.gov/Session/Bill/2022/7

Iowa Legislative Services Agency. (2023). *Iowa legislature – BillBook*. Iowa.gov. www.legis.iowa.gov/legislation/BillBook?ba=HF802&ga=89

Kingkade, T. (2022, November 16). Moms for liberty-backed school board members fire superintendent, ban critical race theory. *NBC News*. www.nbcnews.com/news/us-news/moms-liberty-berkeley-county-school-board-superintendent-rcna57528

KTAR. (2021, November 10). *After nixing diversity symbols, school district fires leader*. KTAR.com. https://ktar.com/story/4763513/after-nixing-diversity-symbols-school-district-fires-leader/

Maddock, T. (2020, July 29). *How gerrymandering can hurt education*. The Thomas B. Fordham Institute. https://fordhaminstitute.org/national/commentary/how-gerrymandering-can-hurt-education

Moss, A./KFOR. (2022, May 14). *"It's not an issue": El Reno schools superintendent claps back at education secretary over critical race theory*. KFOR.com Oklahoma City. https://

kfor.com/news/local/its-not-an-issue-el-reno-schools-superintendent-claps-back-at-education-secretary-over-critical-race-theory/

Owens, J. (2023, February 1). *Making sense of classroom limitations on race and Gender: A review of the 2022 American Instructional Resources Survey.* New America. Retrieved April 30, 2024, from www.newamerica.org/education-policy/edcentral/making-sense-of-classroom-limitations-on-race-and-gender-a-review-of-the-2022-american-instructional-resources-survey/

Reynolds, K. (2021, June 8). *Iowa legislature – BillBook.* www.legis.iowa.gov/legislation/BillBook?ba=HF802&ga=89

Voter turnout. (2023). FairVote. https://fairvote.org/resources/voter-turnout/

7

Protect Black Students From Racial Trauma

Zahra, Zaire, and Zamorah, I took all of you to a public park in a White neighborhood one Sunday afternoon. Children of all ethnic backgrounds were in the park that day, but most of the children were White. They were there with White caregivers.

All three of you have kind spirits and make friends easily. Zamorah, you began playing with a group of little White girls. Zaire, you joined in, and Zahra, you sat on a bench and played on your iPad.

One of the little White girls fell and hurt herself. I saw when she fell. She tripped over her own feet and fell hard to the ground. She cried at the top of her lungs, and from the ground, she pointed at you, Zaire.

Being caring children, Zamorah and Zaire, you began to comfort the little girl and kept asking, "Are you okay?"

Only one thought went through my head: This little White girl is about to blame Zaire for pushing her to the ground.

Her parents did not see her fall and did not hear her cries. No White adults came immediately to her aid.

Zahra, you saw Zaire and Zamorah trying to calm the little White girl, and you walked over to join them.

DOI: 10.4324/9781003529507-7

I yelled at the top of my lungs, "Zaire, Zamorah, Zahra! Come here, now!

You all left the little White girl crying on the ground and trotted to me.

"Why do you think I called you all over here?" I asked.

"I don't know," all three of you responded.

"Look around you," I said. "How many Black people do you see?"

Zahra, you said, "Hardly any."

Zaire, I asked you if you saw the little White girl pointing at you while she was crying. You said you did, but you wanted to see if she was okay. I explained that the little White girl was pointing at you to accuse you of pushing her down, even though you didn't. I explained that White people sometimes blame Black people for things they didn't do.

"That happens at my school," you told me, Zahra. "White kids hardly ever get in trouble when they break the rules."

My heart broke a little that day.

Zahra, you were only in the third grade, and already you recognized that White kids in your school were treated differently than the Black kids.

This is the kind of lesson about race and discrimination that Black parents often teach Black children. The teachers Black students need probably won't be as unfiltered as I was in this instance. However, it is helpful when teachers recognize race-based discriminatory events, help students process them, and diffuse them. In fact, it is more than helpful. On the right day and at the right moment, helping students understand race-based discrimination can keep children alive, away from harm, and confident in their sense of self.

What Racial Discrimination Looks Like at School and How It Impacts Black Students

It's important to know how racial discrimination negatively affects your Black students and what it looks like so you can respond to it, stop it from happening again, and help your

Black students cope with it. Race-based discrimination can be intentional, like bullying a student because they are Black, or unintentional, like disciplining Black students more frequently and severely due to implicit racial bias. Both forms of discrimination are harmful and prevalent.

In a 2020 study in the *Journal of Applied Developmental Psychology*, Black teenagers 13 to 17 years old reported experiencing racial discrimination five times per day (English et al., 2020), and the number of schools where at least one racial hate crime occurred increased from 543 in 2016 to 1,275 in 2018, a 234 percent increase in two years (Kingkade, 2021).

Students are bullied because of their race more than any other identity factor (Yang & McKnight, 2023). In the 2018–2019 school year, 48 percent of students reported being bullied due to their race. These numbers are likely higher since Black, Indigenous, and people of color (BIPOC) students are less likely to report being bullied (Yang & McKnight, 2023).

Black students experience more racial bullying than other races; Black students account for only 15 percent of all children in public schools, yet they make up 37 percent of students who are bullied at school (Yang & McKnight, 2023). Many Black students experience racial trauma from the cumulative effect of racial discrimination.

Racial trauma can lead to a variety of physical and mental health issues like depression, anxiety, violent behavior, hypertension, cardiovascular disease, eating disorders, and even post-traumatic stress disorder (Murray, 2021). Racial trauma can affect children of color as young as four years old, and its negative impacts on mental and physical health are more severe for African Americans than any other group (*Coping with racial trauma*, n.d.) (Ma, 2023).

Race-based discrimination can manifest in a variety of ways. For instance, it can be verbal in the form of a student or teacher saying a racial slur to a Black student. It's not uncommon for Black students to endure racial epithets at school, but hateful speech negatively impacts all students, not just Black students. A quarter of the 5.2 million students who were bullied in the 2018–2019 school year were bullied for aspects of their identity: their race, national origin, disability, religion, gender, or sexual orientation; 1.6 million of those students experienced hate speech due to their identity, and 800,000 of those students were subjected to hate speech because of their race (Chavez, 2021).

In Grand Prairie, Texas, on March 9, 2023, Dubiski Career High School educators found a video on social media showing Dubiski Career students chanting a racial slur in their classroom. Several students held Post-it notes that said, "I hate n****** 4 life." Dubiski freshman Amaia Davis said (as reported by fox4news.com), "When I saw it [the video], I actually wasn't surprised because every single day it's another racial slur" (Anglin, 2023).

Students who experience hate speech experience difficulty being "fully present and attentive" at school. Eight percent of students who have been called hate-related words stay home from school out of fear of being attacked or harmed by one of their peers. Twenty-seven percent of students called a hate-related word avoided classes, areas of their schools, or school-based activities to avoid hate speech directed at them (*Journal of Blacks in Higher Education*, 2019).

> **Pause and Reflect**
> Are any Black students in your class suffering from race-based discrimination or trauma? To what extent do events in your classroom or school cause this discrimination or trauma? Please share.

Race-based discrimination also happens on social media. In Douglas County, Colorado, race-based bullying occurred for months during the 2022–2023 school year in a Snapchat group (Ettinger, 2023). The group was made up of 100 students from Douglas County School District's high school and middle school. White students posted racial slurs and violent messages like, "We should remove blacks from this planet. Bring back [the] holocaust" and tagged Black students in the group so they would see it. It's race-based discrimination when a student threatens physical violence to students who are Black. In that same Snapchat group, other students wrote that Black students should kill themselves. That's another example of a threat of violence.

Race-based discrimination isn't just among students. When teachers and school staff treat Black students differently from White students for the same actions, that too is race-based discrimination. In the 2022–2023 school year, a teacher reprimanded a 16-year-old biracial girl at Douglas County High School for wearing Nike athletic shorts, telling her it violated the school dress code. The teen pointed out a White girl walking by wearing the same shorts, and the teacher told her, "She [a biracial girl] was not built like other girls" (Ettinger, 2023).

Just because someone isn't threatening violence to a Black person doesn't mean that their racially insensitive behavior isn't violent. All racially insensitive behavior is violent. Race-based bullying and discrimination alienates, humiliates, scares, and scars students; these behaviors have no place in schools. The teachers Black students need respond aggressively to race-based violence when they discover it because Black students also deserve to receive a rigorous education at a school campus where they belong and feel safe and supported.

How to Respond to Race-Based Bullying in Your Classroom

Students should not have to endure bullying of any kind. Bullying is never okay and must always be immediately addressed. When you see race-based bullying, redirect the behavior instantly. The moment you hear or see it, stop teaching, publicly call it out, and say, "That's not acceptable. We don't do that in our class, and we don't do that in our school." Be mindful that White students are not the only students who may bully others because of their race. BIPOC students can bully other BIPOC students because of their race too.

After publicly acknowledging the bullying and explaining how it was unacceptable, pull the student who engaged in bullying aside, explain why their behavior was hurtful and offensive, and refer them to a school administrator. Call the offending student's family to tell them what happened and let them know a school administrator may contact them about their child's conduct. It is also wise to call the family of the student who was bullied to inform them of the racially insensitive behavior their child experienced. By taking these steps, you can work toward creating a safe and supportive environment for everyone in your classroom.

It is important that you always report race-based bullying because you don't know if the bullying is a recurring behavior for the offending student, especially in secondary school. You may see race-based bullying in your classroom, but yours is only one out of six the student attends, and the offending student may be bullying students in multiple class periods or may have been bullying students based on their race for years. If you don't report the behavior, the need for intervention, redirection, or consequences may go unnoticed.

If you see racial bullying right before a transition like lunch or students going to another class, you still must address it. Even if you witness it right as students leave your classroom, tell them, "This offensive behavior is unacceptable. We will address this tomorrow. The racially offensive behavior has no place in our class." At the start of the following class, reinforce that what happened was harmful and unacceptable behavior in your classroom and won't be tolerated.

> **Pause and Reflect**
> What steps can you take to disrupt race-based hate or bullying in schools? What action steps resonate with you? Please share.
>
> _____
> _____
> _____

If you notice that a racially insensitive incident impacts your whole class, disrupting students' ability to learn and your ability to teach, stop teaching altogether. Immediately address the student who bullied their peer, and help your students process and heal. You may say, "Class, I need to bring us together to discuss what happened to one of our classmates and what might have been insensitive to you." Create a safe space for the kids impacted, but don't force them to talk. It may be prudent to ask a counselor to come into your class to help you address the behavior and how it affected your classroom.

With the support of a counselor, consider using restorative practices like restorative circles or justice tribunals to respond to race-based bullying. Restorative practices are conflict resolution strategies that involve everyone involved and focus on repairing the harm that has been done; they are helpful when a student's choices disrupt an entire class community. For trust to be rebuilt, the harm a student commits needs to be acknowledged and reconciled.

Restorative circles are one of many restorative practices. Restorative circles are group dialogues that help students resolve conflicts by holding each other accountable, acknowledging participants' feelings, and honoring participants' needs. Restorative justice tribunals are another restorative practice. They are a simple yet comprehensive reflection process for teachers and students. They allow students to have a voice, clear misunderstandings, see how their actions affect their school community, and allow those who commit harm to repair it. I explain how to implement both restorative practices in the book *Restorative Justice Tribunal: And Ways to Derail Jim Crow Discipline in Schools*.

Do not let harassment and discrimination go unchecked. If you witness race-based bullying in your classroom and don't acknowledge it, you communicate to your BIPOC students that your classroom isn't a safe space for them and that you don't care enough about them to make it one. Your inactions also communicate that you won't advocate for their education and that racial discrimination and bullying are okay in your classroom. Racial microaggressions, even when they're unintentional, can also be traumatic for your Black students. To learn how to respond to microaggressions in your classroom, refer to Chapter Three. Every student deserves to attend school in a safe and respectful learning environment.

Use Professional Judgment to Discern How to Respond to Racially Insensitive Behavior

How do you know when racial discrimination or insensitivity needs the immediate attention of your administrator? Use your professional judgment.

For example, some Black students are okay with their White friends calling them the N-word. While these students may be okay with that behavior, it does not make it right or appropriate in schools. In this situation, you can stop the students and say, "What you just said isn't okay. We don't say that in my classroom." If the Black student responds, "They're my friend. It's okay. I'm not offended." You can respond, "I understand your feelings, but that language is never okay in my class. You may be okay with hearing the N-word from your friend, but other students who overhear it may not be. Even if they're okay with it, I'm not okay with it."

Even when Black students say they're not offended when their peers call them the N-word, the behavior is still not appropriate. The N-word is a derogatory word used to belittle and dehumanize Black people. In this situation, you may not feel a need to report the incident to your administrator, but it's important to call the student's parents and let them know that they said the N-word in your class.

Similarly, if two Black students were casually using the N-word with each other without any intention to cause harm, you would let them know that saying the N-word is not appropriate in your classroom and would call their parents to let them know that they used that word in your class. There wouldn't be a need to report the incident to your administrator unless harm was intended. Use your professional judgment to decide.

If you witness incidents involving racial bullying in or outside your classroom, immediately call your administrator to address it. If you see students of different ethnicities hurling racial epithets at each other, threatening violence, or making racist jokes, call an administrator for immediate support.

> **Pause and Reflect**
>
> Do you feel safe to disrupt race-based hate or bullying in your classroom or school? If not, what makes you hesitant? Please share.
>
> _____
> _____
> _____

How to Respond When Racial Trauma in the Community Affects Your Class

What's insidious about racial trauma is that it can affect your students indirectly, too (*How to Recognize and Cope with Racial Trauma*, 2020). Repeated exposure to racially discriminatory behavior in the media can cause distress and trauma for Black students. In recent years, the media has been covering violence against Black people more frequently, especially law enforcement-involved shootings. Black students are exposed to violent headlines, images, and viral videos of Black people being murdered on the news and social media – a space they can't filter. Exposure to that once, let alone repeated exposure, can traumatize Black students.

In 2022, over 300 Black people were killed by police (*Mapping Police Violence*, n.d.). That translates to law enforcement killing a Black person every day for ten months straight, and the majority of victims were men. In any given month, if you search the internet for "Black man killed by a police officer" and click "News," you'll find a list of new names of Black people killed after being pulled over for a traffic stop, mental health check, or domestic dispute call because that's how the majority of Black killings by police begin (*Mapping Police Violence*, n.d.).

In August of 2023, Ricky Cobb II, a 33-year-old Black man, was shot and killed after being pulled over for a broken taillight in Minneapolis, Minnesota ("Family of Ricky Cobb II, Black Man Fatally Shot During Traffic Stop, Calls for Troopers Involved to Be Fired," 2023). In Indianapolis, Indiana, three days after Cobb was killed, police used deadly force on 49-year-old Gary Harrell, a Black man whom police shot in the back and killed when he ran after being pulled over for a traffic violation (Howell & White, 2023). Two days later, police used deadly force when responding to a domestic violence call where they shot and killed Brandon Cole, a 36-year-old Black man in Denver, Colorado, mistaking the black marker he was holding for a knife (Beaty, 2023).

Racially discriminatory behavior often appears in the media, and not just regarding police-involved shootings of Black people. In Kansas City, Missouri, on April 13, 2023, 16-year-old Black teenager Ralph Yarl went to the wrong house to pick up his twin brothers. When he rang the doorbell, he was shot twice (Zaru & Ghebremedhin, 2023). On June 2, 2023, Ajike Owens, a 35-year-old Black woman, went to confront her neighbor for yelling racial slurs and throwing a pair of skates at her kids, hitting one of them ("Black Florida Mother Killed by White Neighbor Remembered for Faith, Devotion to 4 Kids | AP News," 2023). She knocked on her neighbor's door with her nine-year-old son beside her. Her neighbor shot her twice without opening the door, killing her.

Since Trayvon Martin, a 17-year-old Black teenager, was killed 11 years ago while walking home from a store for looking "suspicious," over 18,000 more people have been killed due to stand-your-ground laws (Buncombe, 2022). The majority of the victims were Black. Stand-your-ground laws state that you can use deadly force as an act of self-defense when you believe your life is in danger.

Headlines of White people calling the police on Black people for doing mundane things are also common. Two Black men were arrested for trespassing while sitting in Starbucks in Philadelphia, Pennsylvania (Winsor & McCarthy, 2018). In Lansing, Michigan, Tashawn Bernard, a 12-year-old Black boy, was put in handcuffs and detained while walking to his apartment after taking out the trash (Duster, 2023). Dayson Barnes, a Black man, moved to Seattle from Texas with the hope of escaping frequent racial profiling while walking or jogging in his neighborhood. Three weeks after moving to Seattle, one of his neighbors called the police after seeing Dayson in his backyard and reported that he broke in and was stealing . . . from his own house (AP News, 2022).

Although stories of Black people being policed, shot, and killed for existing are common, these news stories don't always negatively impact your students to the extent that they disrupt their ability to learn. So how do you know when you need to stop teaching so you can address the trauma your students are experiencing and support them? Teaching is an art and a science, so sometimes you'll feel it. You'll just know when it is time to pause and attend to the socio-emotional health of your students.

Think about the events surrounding the unfortunate, unnecessary, and tragic death of George Floyd. When George Floyd was murdered, the video of his death went viral with the hashtag #BlackLivesMatter. His death affected people around the globe, and the world took to the streets in protest, including students at schools. George Floyd's death was everywhere – in the news, on social media, and in people's mouths as a topic of conversation. It was a constant retraumatization for many African Americans.

When George Floyd was murdered, some teachers had to stop teaching the standards to provide a safe space for students to process and heal from the tragic events; some students needed help processing the racial trauma they were experiencing. It was important that teachers helped them because trauma shuts down parts of the brain associated with concentration, memory, learning, and emotional regulation, making it harder for students to learn (Yump Digital, n.d.). When you see that news of racial violence disrupts your classroom community, it's important to acknowledge the harm surrounding the event and provide a safe space for your students to talk about it.

Pause and Reflect

Do you know of a race-based incident that occurred in your community or the community of one of your Black students that spilled over into your school? If so, what happened? Please share.

_____
_____
_____

If a current event is not disruptive to your class and your students don't seem impacted by it, don't make it an issue. Some students may say they want to talk about an event, but if it's not preventing you from teaching the standards, then teach the standards. Refer the student who asked to talk about the event to a school counselor for support. If several students express that racial violence or racial discrimination in the media concerns them, then address it directly. Even then, you must be mindful of how much instructional time you use to help your students process and heal. Don't hesitate to enlist the support of a school counselor if needed.

I want to acknowledge that every educator is not professionally equipped to help students process emotionally challenging moments. You may not be comfortable talking about racial insensitivity with your students. That's okay, and you should not feel bad about your discomfort. It's a myth that because someone is a teacher, they'll automatically be good at having difficult conversations with students. It's okay to call school counselors or a school administrator for support during these moments. Don't beat yourself up or feel bad about not having the tools or skills to help your kids work through trauma or deeply personal emotional struggles they may have. You weren't trained to do that, but school counselors, psychologists, and social workers are.

How to Respond to Race-Based Discrimination in School Hallways

When you're outside of your classroom in spaces like hallways, the lunchroom, or the school parking lot, you're in a less controlled environment, which makes it harder to disrupt race-based bullying and discrimination. Transitions between classes can also be hectic. With a packed schedule, you likely use most of your breaks to catch up on work, fine-tune lessons, grade, or use the bathroom. All of these circumstances can make it challenging for you to address race-based bullying or racial insensitivity outside of the classroom.

Although challenging, it's essential to immediately disrupt race-based hate, ignorance, or bias whenever you see it. Address it outside of the classroom as you would inside of the classroom. Instantly acknowledge and redirect the behavior. Say to the offending students, "That behavior is unacceptable. We don't do or say that in our school." Then, report the behavior to an administrator.

If a class is about to start when you witness race-based bullying or racially insensitive behavior, ask a colleague to watch your students so you can intervene, such as a teacher in the class next to you or a campus safety monitor. If you need more support, call your administrator for help. It's vital to stop race-based bullying and discrimination as soon as you see it to set the tone for the culture that you want on your campus.

How to Respond to Race-Based Discrimination From a Colleague

Adults in schools may exhibit racial insensitivity unknowingly or intentionally. It is common to believe that educators' love of children and self-actualization would prompt them to treat others fairly and respectfully, at least more consistently than non-educators. Unfortunately, this does not appear to be the case.

Researchers in *Educational Researcher* in 2020 compared teachers' implicit and explicit racial biases with those of non-educators. Seventy-seven percent of teachers and 77.1 percent of non-teachers showed implicit racial bias, and 30.3 percent of teachers and 30.4 percent of non-teachers demonstrated explicit racial bias. The results were essentially the same.

Because everyone has implicit biases, you may witness one of your colleagues racially discriminate against a Black student during your career. If you ever witness a teacher bullying a student because of their race, report them immediately. Teachers who bully and intentionally harm students have no place in this profession.

In September 2023, a Black eighth-grader, new to Sedgwick Middle School in West Hartford, Connecticut, was excited to start the school year. Three days into his first week, his math teacher was reviewing the classroom policy, going over profane language not allowed in the classroom. He asked his teacher to clarify what she meant by profane language that wasn't cursing. She said the N-word.

"You don't even know what it means," she told her students, who were surprised by her language, as reported by NBC Connecticut. "It means 'my slave'" (Howard, 2023). She continued, "Yeah, well, I know you guys are shocked that I said it. I said it, and I can say it because I'm a teacher. You guys can't because you're students." She said the N-word multiple times, directing it at the new Black student, assuming it was a word he used often. The next day, his mother reported the incident to the district. If a student tells you that one of your colleagues said the N-word or you overhear a colleague saying it, report the teacher. No one, including teachers, should say the N-word. I know it's scary and difficult to report a colleague, but it's the right thing to do.

Rather than bullying, you're more likely to see instances of implicit racial discrimination relating to grading, dress codes, discipline, or how teachers talk about Black students and their parents. An equity consultant recalled her first years as a public high school administrator in Illinois, witnessing how White and Black students were treated differently for wearing sagging jeans in the hallway, a violation of the school dress code (Hurst, 2016). A teacher called her over and was berating a Black student for sagging his pants. The teacher asked her to take him to the discipline office to "fix him."

As she walked the student to the office, he pointed out four other boys with their pants sagging. All of them were White, and no teachers stopped or scolded them. Instead, teachers were engaged in friendly conversations with them. She told the Black student to wait for her before entering the office at the end of the hallway. She walked to one of the White boys with sagging jeans who was conversing with a teacher and said, "What's up with those pants, young man?" The teacher kindly told the White student, "Look at you. Pull those up, would you?" After the student pulled his pants up, the teacher turned to her and said, "See? Wasn't that easy? All we have to do is ask them."

Often, Black students aren't given that same respect or opportunity. If you witness an incident like this, know the teacher, and have a relationship with them, talk to your colleague directly. Tell them what they did or said is not okay and explain why. Give examples of how they could have handled the situation differently. For example, if a student's pants are sagging, they could ask them to pull them up. If they don't see any reason to call out White students for a dress code infraction, push back on their thinking and ask them if there's any need to discipline Black students for the same thing.

Racial discrimination between teachers and students can happen without students being present. You may overhear a comment in the teacher lounge or be a part of a conversation when a colleague shares racialized statements about Black students or parents.

A 2022 peer-reviewed study published in *Urban Education* looked at coded racialized communication among educators at an urban high school in the Midwest (Marcucci & Elmesky, 2022). Coded racialized communication is when people communicate racial ideas, often related to negative stereotypes, without explicitly using racial words. In the study, many examples of coded racialized communication were noted, including two White teachers talking about how the school's Black parents didn't care about their children.

The teachers joked, pretending to be Black parents (Marcucci & Elmesky, n.d.).

One teacher said, "Yeah, just somebody saying, 'Hey, you know you have a baby, right?'"

"I do?" the other responded.

"Yeah."

"Oh, wooord," the teacher said, using stereotypical African American vernacular.

The study noted that White teachers who acknowledged that their Black students experienced systemic racism still often used stereotypes when talking about them and their families, even teachers who pushed back against racial stereotypes. Many teachers are not intentionally trying to cause harm or stereotype their students. Instead, they're unaware that they're doing it.

If you're in a conversation with a colleague, and they make a statement that racializes Black students or parents, you can gently call them out on it. For example, you could say something like, "Hey, John Doe. I want to gently push back on what you said about our Black parents not caring about their kids," and then explain why that's a harmful stereotype. If you have a more comfortable relationship with that colleague, you could explain how their belief may create an unintentional barrier to connecting with Black parents.

If you don't have a relationship with the teacher and don't feel comfortable approaching them, go to your administrator or a trusted colleague and ask them to talk to the educator who behaved disrespectfully. Recommend staff professional development on unconscious bias, microaggressions, and racial insensitivity. To stay silent is to be complicit. While it's hard, you have to say something because that's how one interrupts racial discrimination, hate, and bias.

It's vital to call out implicit racial bias and discrimination from other educators because if they're unaware of what they're doing and the negative impact they're having, they'll continue to do it.

How to Support Students Who Tell You They're Being Racially Bullied or Discriminated Against

If a student confides in you that they're being racially bullied or discriminated against, it's because they trust you. Stay calm and composed when discussing the incident with the student, even if you find it abhorrent. It's important to center your students' feelings and experiences to give them the space to express their emotions. If you react from an emotionally charged place, you'd be centering your feelings and taking away that opportunity for your students.

Giving your Black students time and space to feel seen and heard can help them cope with racial trauma and aggression. Actively listen to your student's perspective and seek to understand how the incident made them feel. Reflect back what your student tells you and ask if you understand them correctly: "I heard that [X action] makes you feel unwelcome at this school. Did I get that right?" Validate your student's feelings: "I'm sorry you had to experience that. That sounds frustrating, exhausting, and upsetting."

In addition to validating your students' feelings, thank them for opening up to you. "I can see why you would feel like that. Thank you for sharing this with me." Empathetic recognition – recognizing and connecting with another's vulnerability and suffering – is essential to healing. You could also recommend school resources that may help your student process their racial experiences further. School-based clubs such as a Black student union or multicultural club allow students to support one another and stand up against racial insensitivity. Spaces where Black students can process racial experiences are therapeutic, and they can help students recognize and avoid racial insensitivity and racially hostile situations.

Educators who engage with students in these spaces become trusted adults with whom students can speak about many things, including incidents of racial insensitivity. These spaces provide opportunities for educators to listen to students, validate their feelings, and help them navigate the fear and frustration associated with race-based bullying and racial insensitivity.

"Nobody's Listening!" How to Respond to Students' Concerns about Racial Discrimination When They Feel Ignored

Sometimes, adults disregard Black students' concerns and ignore their complaints about racial insensitivity and bullying. Unfortunately, this reaction from teachers and leadership isn't uncommon, and it creates unsafe spaces for Black students that are unsuitable for learning.

In 2019, the Davis School District in Utah was investigated by the Department of Justice for ignoring hundreds of racial harassment complaints against Black and Asian-American students (Chavez, 2021). In 2022, five students from Ankeny Centennial High School testified at a school district board meeting that they reported racism they experienced from students and teachers on multiple occasions, but their concerns were ignored. Three Black and biracial families filed a federal lawsuit against Douglas County Schools in 2023 for failing to protect their kids from racial discrimination from staff and daily racial slurs, insults, and threats of violence from students (Brundin, 2023).

Retaliation is also a common experience for students who report racial discrimination and bullying. A student from Effingham County School District (ECSD) transferred after his school retaliated against him for reporting racist SnapChats where White students threatened to "assassinate" and "execute" "N******." Once he transferred, ECSD held back his transcripts for months, and once they sent them, his transcripts had false infractions on them, and his grades were changed from As to Cs (Payne, 2023).

When students tell you that their complaints about racial discrimination and bullying are being ignored, give them your full attention, actively listen, intervene, and use the reporting mechanisms outlined in your school or district policies to inform leaders. Schools typically have policies prohibiting discrimination, harassment, and bullying, as well as policies to inform administrators when people direct racial slurs at others or subject them to race-based bullying. It's important to uphold these policies. If racial discrimination and bullying go unchecked, it can become rampant, making your school unsafe for Black students.

If pathways to reporting discriminatory behavior don't exist in your school or district, which is rare, send correspondence to your school leader, anonymous or otherwise. Include their supervisor if needed. If after you make leaders aware of racially insensitive behavior and if change still does not appear to happen, report students' concerns to your local branch of the National Association for the Advancement of Colored People (NAACP), the American Civil Liberties Union, the Anti-Defamation League, or other advocacy organizations.

It can be scary to go outside of your school to report issues that aren't being dealt with. Retaliation is a valid fear, but know that federal law protects you from retaliation for coming forward with information (*Whistleblower Protections*, n.d.). Every student deserves to go to school in a safe and respectful learning environment. While it may feel scary to tell an outside entity, anonymously or not, that students are experiencing racially insensitive behavior at school, your Black students need you.

3-2-1 Chapter Reflection

Take a moment to reflect on the content of the chapter and what it means to you.

What are three important ideas from this chapter?

_____
_____
_____

What are two action steps you can take based on this chapter?
_____
_____
_____

What is one concept you would like to explore in more depth?
_____
_____
_____

References

Anglin, D. (2023, March 23). Grand Prairie NAACP calls for students using racial slurs in video to be expelled. *FOX 4*. www.fox4news.com/news/grand-prairie-students-dubiski-career-high-school-racial-slurs

Beaty, K. (2023, August 16). Brandon Cole's killing by Denver Police leaves advocates waiting to see how a new mayor will respond – and if anything will change. *Denverite*. https://denverite.com/2023/08/16/brandon-cole-denver-police-shooting-mike-johnston/

Black Florida mother killed by white neighbor remembered for faith, devotion to 4 kids. (2023, June 12). *AP News*. https://apnews.com/article/neighbor-shooting-florida-manslaughter-6986f11d0aeed6a9aaf147354ae85c1c

Brundin, J. (2023, August 3). *Lawsuit alleges Douglas County School District failed to protect students from racial harassment*. Colorado Public Radio. https://www.cpr.org/2023/08/02/douglas-county-school-district-lawsuit-student-racism-harassment/

Buncombe, A. (2022, February 26). After Trayvon Martin, up to 18,000 killed under "racist" stand-your-ground laws. *The Independent*. www.independent.co.uk/news/world/americas/trayvon-martin-anniversary-stand-your-ground-law-b2023978.html

CNN, N. C. (n.d.). *A Utah school district ignored hundreds of racial harassment complaints against Black and Asian American students, DOJ says.* CNN. www.cnn.com/2021/10/22/us/utah-school-district-ignored-racial-harassment-doj/index.html

Coping with racial trauma. (n.d.). *The department of psychology.* Psychology.uga.edu. https://psychology.uga.edu/coping-racial-trauma

Duster, C. (2023, August 15). *Father of a 12-year-old detained while taking out trash says he will not accept a police apology.* CNN. www.cnn.com/2023/08/15/us/tashawn-bernard-father-rejects-police-apology-cnntv/index.html

English, D., Lambert, S. F., Tynes, B. M., Bowleg, L., Zea, M. C., & Howard, L. C. (2020). Daily multidimensional racial discrimination among Black U.S. American adolescents. *Journal of Applied Developmental Psychology, 66,* 101068. https://doi.org/10.1016/j.appdev.2019.101068

Ettinger, M. (2023, August 11). Snapchat group with 100 students tagged Black kids in racial slurs, fueled racism at middle school, lawsuit alleges. *The Daily Dot.* www.dailydot.com/debug/castle-rock-middle-school-snapchat-lawsuit/

Family of Ricky Cobb II, Black man fatally shot during traffic stop, calls for troopers involved to be fired. (2023, August 3). *CBS News.* www.cbsnews.com. www.cbsnews.com/news/ricky-cobb-family-black-man-killed-traffic-stop-wants-troopers-shot-him-fired-charged/

Howard, B. L. (2023, September 20). Public blasts do-nothing school after teacher's racial slur. *Yahoo News.* https://news.yahoo.com/public-blasts-nothing-school-teacher-212354759.html

Howell, J., Jr., & White, J. (2023, August 22). *IMPD releases bodycam footage of August shooting, killing 49-year-old Gary Harrell.* WRTV Indianapolis. www.wrtv.com/news/local-news/crime/impd-releases-video-summary-of-august-shooting-killing-49-year-old-gary-harrell

Hurst, K. W. (2016, December 7). *Biased discipline at my school.* Edutopia. www.edutopia.org/article/biased-discipline-at-my-school-kelly-wickham-hurst/

Journal of Blacks in Higher Education. (2019, November 4). How hate-speech at school can lead to poor academic outcomes. *The Journal of Blacks in Higher Education.* https://jbhe.com/2019/11/how-hate-speech-at-school-can-lead-to-poor-academic-outcomes/

Kingkade, T. (2021, December 16). As parents protest critical race theory, students fight racist behavior at school. *NBC News.* www.nbcnews.com/news/us-news/critical-race-theory-student-protests-rcna8926

Ma, A. (2023, May 23). Racism starts before kids even start school, causing a major mental health crisis. An AP series explores the mental health impacts of racism faced by black children. *AP NEWS.* https://projects.apnews.com/features/2023/from-birth-to-death/mental-health-black-children-investigation.html

Marcucci, O., & Elmesky, R. M. (2022). Coded racialized discourse among educators: Implications for social-emotional outcomes and cultures of antiblackness at an urban school. *Urban Education*, 004208592211191. https://doi.org/10.1177/00420859221119115

Marcucci, O., & Elmesky, R. (n.d.). White teachers often talk about Black students in racially coded ways. *The Conversation.* https://theconversation.com/white-teachers-often-talk-about-black-students-in-racially-coded-ways-190814

Murray, R. (2021, June 24). *What is racial trauma? How Black therapists are helping patients cope.* TODAY.com. www.today.com/health/what-racial-trauma-how-black-therapists-are-helping-patients-cope-t184880

Payne, B. (2023, January 18). *Lawsuit: Georgia school district lowered Black student's GPA after he reported racist Snapchats.* Georgia Public Broadcasting. www.gpb.org/news/2023/01/18/lawsuit-georgia-school-district-lowered-black-students-gpa-after-he-reported-racist

Racial trauma: What it is and how to cope. (2020, December 21). *Healthline.* www.healthline.com/health/mental-health/racial-trauma#whos-affected

Sinyangwe, S. (2023). Mapping Police Violence. https://mappingpoliceviolence.us/

U.S. Department of Labor. (2023). *Whistleblower protections.* U.S. Department of Labor. www.dol.gov. www.dol.gov/general/topics/whistleblower

White woman calls police on Black man standing at his home. (2022, August 6). *AP News.* https://apnews.com/article/race-and-ethnicity-racial-injustice-seattle-african-americans-3bfdd7f5c7bfd9fca701c10f40c42672

Winsor, M., & McCarthy, K. (2018, April 20). Men arrested at Starbucks were there for business meeting hoping to change 'our lives'. *ABC News.* https://abcnews.go.com/GMA/News/men-arrested-starbucks-business-meeting-hoping-change-lives/story?id=54578217

Yang, Y., & McKnight, J. (2023, April 28). Students of color are disproportionately bullied and harassed at school. *Public Health Post.* https://publichealthpost.org/health-equity/students-of-color-are-disproportionately-bullied-and-harassed-at-school/

Yump. (2020, June 8). *How childhood trauma affects learning and . . .* MacKillop Family Services. www.mackillop.org.au/stories/how-childhood-trauma-affects-learning-and-how-to-help-children-overcome-it#:~:text=Children%20and%20young%20people%20who

Zaru, D., & Ghebremedhin, S. (2023, June 27). Ralph Yarl, teen shot after mistakenly going to the wrong house, opens up about recovery in "GMA" exclusive. *ABC News.* https://abcnews.go.com/US/ralph-yarl-teen-shot-after-mistakenly-wrong-house/story?id=100385425

8

Black Students' Relationship With School Police

Zahra, Zaire, and Zamorah, often you overheard me talking with school police officers, coordinating how we would keep students and staff safe. Once, gang members kicked in the door of a student's house, shot at family members (fortunately missing them), and ran. Several of the young men were students in my high school.

School Police Officer MacGruder called me at home to tell me what had happened in the neighborhood that night. We were both concerned about retaliation on campus the following day, so we discussed what we needed to do to keep the campus safe for the rest of the week. Fortunately, we ended the week without incident.

Shortly after the dismissal bell that Friday, Detective Pearson from the North Las Vegas gang unit called me. Detective Pearson told me the word on the street was that a rival gang member was looking for one of my students who shot up the house and planned to shoot him at the football game that Friday night. We were glad we were the "away" team, and the game was off campus. The opposing school did not have many gang-affiliated students.

Four officers were in Detective Pearson's gang unit. Two of his men looked young, so they were going to be undercover that night

DOI: 10.4324/9781003529507-8

at the game. Pearson asked me to give him two Cheyenne t-shirts so his officers could blend in with the crowd, which I did. Officer Mac-Gruder was working the game that night, too, which was good. He knew the names and faces of students who were persons of interest. I went to the game that night, too, and I was on edge from start to finish, scanning the crowd for trouble.

Zahra, you asked me if you, your brother, and your sister could go to the game with me, and I told you no. I never took you three to away football games anyway, and there was too much to be concerned about that night. Nothing problematic happened at the stadium that night. The problem happened in the parking lot.

During the game, the police detained a car and its passengers because the car reeked of marijuana. Two of the young men in the car were affiliated with the gang seeking payback for shooting at the house earlier that week. When the police searched the car, they found two loaded handguns.

Students Want to Feel Safe at School

The push for more school police officers began as an attempt to prevent school violence, particularly school shootings. This was understandable after the 1999 gun-related tragedy at Columbine High School in Littleton, Colorado, that kickstarted a frightening new culture. Now, every few months we expect to hear about a school shooting on the news and see the images of dead children and educators on our TV screens that follow.

While most school communities won't experience a tragedy like Marjory Stoneman Douglas High School or Sandy Hook Elementary School, more than a quarter of schools will experience a gun-related lockdown, and it's more prevalent for high schools in urban areas. During the 2022–2023 school year, 34 percent of high school educators reported at least one gun-related lockdown (Hurst, 2024).

The threat of a school shooting is a fear that lingers in teachers' minds today. According to a 2023 national survey,

59 percent of public K–12 teachers expressed worry about a school shooting at their campus, and students are concerned, too (Hurst, 2024). Fifty-seven percent of students ages 13 to 17 worry about the possibility of a school shooting, according to a 2018 study, and in the 2022 State of School Safety Report, an active shooter was students' number one school safety concern (Graf, 2024) (Safe and Sound Schools, Raptor Technologies, & Lightspeed Systems, 2022).

With the threat of gun violence looming over schools, students and educators want to feel safe and secure on their campuses, and school districts across the country are debating whether school resource officers are the answer. According to a 2023 study, school resource officers' presence at schools reduces threats, fights without weapons, and sexual assault but does not prevent gun violence (Sorensen & Avila-Acosta, 2023). When it comes to feeling safe at school, some students feel safer with police officers at their schools, but that sense of safety differs by the race of the students.

In the 2017–2018 school year, thousands of California high school students were surveyed across eight diverse, low-income school districts. Sixty-one percent of White students compared with 41 percent of Black students reported feeling safer with a police officer on campus (Nakamoto et al., 2017). In the 2018–2019 school year, 3,807 sixth- to eleventh-grade students from 21 New Orleans public schools were surveyed about their perceptions of their schools and communities (Bell Weixler et al., 2020). Fifty-three percent said they did not feel safe with police on campus. When asked if they felt safer in their neighborhoods with police present, 69 percent of White students reported feeling safer compared with 40 percent of Black students.

The research isn't conclusive on whether K–12 students feel safe or not with school resource officers present. What the research does show is that White students feel safer than Black students when school officers are on campus, and the majority of Black students don't feel safe with school police on campus.

The schools where I've worked don't match the national data on students' relationships with or sense of safety around school police officers. I've worked at tough schools where gang violence impacted our school communities and spilled onto our campuses. My relationship with the school police force was excellent, and the relationship between the school police and students and families was equally superb.

Our school police prioritized forming and deepening positive relationships with the school community. During lunches, they made small talk with students. They often were the officers on duty at our athletic events, which helped them form positive relationships with athletes, their families, and teachers. The relationships school police had with students, families, and staff were of a nature that school community members called my school's officers directly to warn of potential trouble on campus. When students knew of trouble brewing on campus, they warned Officer MacGruder or his partners.

There is a growing push to remove police officers from school campuses. I don't support that thinking. If the students at schools where I was principal had been asked whether they felt safer on campus with school police, their response would have been a resounding "yes," including my BIPOC students. While my experience with school police was excellent, that is not the case at many schools, especially for Black students and the teachers who teach them.

The Impact of Police on Black Students

While I am a supporter of police on school campuses, it is a fact that police officers on school campuses substantially impact Black students negatively. That was not my experience, but facts are facts. Black students report that police officers watch them more closely than their peers, and that often results in disproportionate disciplining and policing (Ellis, 2022).

Police at schools increase the number of students who receive an out-of-school suspension by 62 percent and the number of expulsions by 90 percent (Sorensen & Avila-Acosta, 2023). Their presence also increases police referrals and student arrests – disproportionately affecting Black students, boys, and students with disabilities (Sorensen & Avila-Acosta, 2023). In 46 states, Black students are referred to law enforcement more than any other student group (Ellis, 2022). Though Black students are 15 percent of public school students, they account for 18 percent of referrals to law enforcement and 22 percent of school-related arrests (U.S. Department of Education, n.d.).

Black students bear the brunt of police violence at schools, as well. More than 80 percent of police violence against students happens to Black students (*Police in Schools Have Outsize Effect on Black Children, Report Says*, 2022). At least 60 percent of those police-on-student assaults caused serious injury: concussions, broken bones, and hospitalizations. Twenty-four police-on-student assaults were sexual assaults, and five caused students' deaths.

Black students' interactions with school police have lasting impacts. Tulane University and the University of Washington did a study of Seattle Public Schools' students to identify the long-term effects of police interactions on Black students. They found that Black students who had contact with the police by eighth grade were 11 times more likely than White students to be arrested when they were 20 years old (Mitchell et al., 2021).

At my school, things went wrong when the police took on the role of teachers. When school police insert themselves in classroom disciplinary matters, or when teachers outsource behavior management to school police officers, the misbehavior that teachers typically handle often gets criminalized (Police in Schools, 2021), and the consequences for Black students have been dire. Hallway scuffles can turn into assault charges, and classroom outbursts can turn into disorderly conduct charges.

In 2019, a school police officer arrested a 6-year-old Black girl for having a temper tantrum. In 2020, police officers in Montgomery County, Maryland, subdued and handcuffed a kindergartener who walked out of school. They screamed at the child at length and declared, "This is why people need to beat their kids" (Ferriss, 2021). In May of 2022, school police placed a child with ADHD in a chokehold and arrested him after he had an outburst.

Teachers would have addressed these behavior infractions had there been no school police on campus. Unfortunately, in these cases, school police officers referred these students to the juvenile justice system (Ellis, 2022). Black students tend to pay a price for the added security that school resource officers provide. It is up to faculty and staff to mitigate Black students' disproportionate referrals to law enforcement.

> **Pause and Reflect**
> Do you have police officers in your school? Do they have positive relationships with students and staff? Please share.
> _____
> _____
> _____

How to Work With School Police to Create a Better Experience for Your Black Students

1. *Know your role and the role of the school police.* The teachers Black students need understand that school police officers should not wade into addressing classroom behaviors, such as tardiness, dress code infractions, and mouthiness in class. School police should not intercede from a law enforcement perspective when students talk when the teacher is trying to

teach, walk to the bathroom without a hall pass, or chew gum in class when it isn't allowed. There are fewer opportunities for school policing to go south if they limit their interactions to infractions of the law.

Classroom management and addressing behavioral issues on campus aren't the role of school police officers. You are responsible for upholding behavioral expectations in your classroom, and when you need support, it's the role of educational staff and the administration to intervene. When teachers outsource their classroom management to school police officers, Black students are disproportionately referred to law enforcement and disproportionately arrested. That's why it's important to know when and when not to call on the support of school resource officersIf a student isn't following directions, sitting in their seat, or being quiet, those aren't reasons to call on the help of your school resource officers. If a student refuses to stop cursing at one of their classmates or is being disrespectful to you, those aren't reasons to ask for their support either. School administrative staff should intervene for these behavioral infractionsIf kids are fighting in class, you should call the school police. They will come in and break it up, but even then, they shouldn't always take students to the school police office. Instead, they should be taken to a school administrator's office. A school fight shouldn't automatically be a reason for students to be put into police custody.

Not all school police know their role when it comes to school discipline. When they do and tell you what they can and can't do regarding student behavior, respect their boundaries and role. At the school I worked at, this is how school resource officers would have responded when they were asked to help with school discipline matters, and it's how school police should respond.

If a teacher asked a school police officer to help them with a classroom management issue, the police officer would call the administrator or hall monitor and relay something like, "Ms. Johnson is asking for assistance in her class for students not complying," but they wouldn't get involved. They might linger outside of the classroom, just in case the situation turned violent or threatening, but rest assured their first call was to school administrative staff.

If an officer heard a kid going off and saw a situation escalating in a class, they might enter the classroom, call the administrator, and be a physical presence, but they would not intervene. Even if the teacher asked them to remove the kid from their class, they wouldn't intervene other than calling the administrator for support unless the situation turned violent or put the class's safety at risk.

If a student doesn't comply with a teacher's and administrator's directions and becomes volatile, the police can intervene. Still, that police intervention doesn't have to result in the student being charged with a crime or detained in the school police office.

The officers in your school should be a liaison between your school, law enforcement, and the surrounding community. Assisting with law enforcement matters on your school campus is the root of good school policing: keeping your school and classroom safe from intruders, addressing juvenile crime and drug-related activity in and around your school, and responding to off-campus criminal behavior involving students. School policing done right doesn't look like enforcing school-based behavior rules because that's not the school police's role, although that's the experience of many students, particularly Black students.

The police at my school rarely got involved in general student disorder. If students were milling about between classes, loitering, or not going to class, our school police officers would say "Let's go! Let's get to class." That's it. Because of their relationships with students, and the obvious authority they had as police officers, students complied. If students mouthed back to them, which rarely happened, school police weren't quick to respond aggressively.

When they did respond to students' mouthiness or disrespectful comments toward them, they escorted students to school administrators, not to the school police office. If students challenged them, they didn't react like aggressive police on the streets. They were much more patient. That's what the behavior of school police should look like.

Cops only intervened at my school when situations got bad. Officers would break up fights, but they wouldn't always charge fighters, unless the students clearly, unquestionably resisted their commands or if the fight clearly, unquestionably escalated to severe levels of disruption. Roughly a third of the fights on campus that officers broke up resulted in school-level discipline, not charges.

2. *Be cordial*. Be cordial and collegial to school police, and model that students can talk to them. Say hi. Talk to them, and get to know them like you would your educator colleagues when you see them on campus and after school at sporting events. Treat school police officers as members of the school community, not add-ons. School resource officers have a stake in the community, and students won't think that if teachers and staff view them as outsiders.

If teachers are afraid to approach school police or choose not to say anything to them, even a hello, then the ability to stop problems before they start diminishes. Being friendly with the school police creates opportunities to help kids and ensure all students stay on a positive path.

3. *Collaborate with school police to stop problems before they start.* You know your students. You know your students who are learning English, who are unhoused, who aren't getting enough to eat, and who are going through something difficult at home. You know which of your students have IEPs. You know your students who have ADHD who sometimes act without thinking, interrupt others, or have difficulty following directions. You know your autistic students who may start shouting, shut down, or physically lash out when overwhelmed. You know what sets them off and how to help them de-escalate. You know how to support your students best. When appropriate, share the information that you have about your students with your school resource officers.

   If a school police officer knows that English is a student's second language, then they know that the student isn't being disrespectful when they don't respond to them; instead, they may just not understand them.

   Suppose a school resource officer knows that a student with autism gets physically aggressive when overwhelmed. In that case, they can use de-escalation strategies to support the student in either preventing that behavior or helping them to de-escalate the behavior when they're experiencing it, instead of escalating it.

   You know your students who get in fights or belong to gangs and who would benefit from adult support to stay out of trouble. Communicate this info to your school resource officers. When I was a school principal, I had a student who was known for fighting on campus. To look at her and interact with her, you never would have known that she had the proclivity to fight. She addressed adults on campus as Ma'am and Sir. She was never truant from school or class and had a delightful personality. But in spite of her delightfulness, she found herself in conflicts with her peers. She was a member of a local gang.

One of my school police officers knew this and had built a relationship with her. He helped her avoid confrontations on campus. During almost every lunch period, he told her he was glad she was at school and glad she was going to class. He coached her on how to avoid conflicts on campus and how to avoid confrontations with young ladies from rival gangs. Unfortunately, one day, she got into a fight during lunch.

The officer intervened, grabbed her by the arm and shoulder, and marched her to the school police office, which was close to where the fight occurred. As they walked, he lectured her like a father, and every few steps, she said, "I'm sorry! I'm sorry," repeatedly apologizing for disappointing the school police officer with whom she had built a relationship.

Through collaboration with my school police officers, they built relationships with students who were gang members, on probation, or just naughty at school and helped them stay on track. When students sometimes fell off the path, they still had good relationships with the school resource officers and didn't want to disappoint them, which encouraged them to try to stay on track.

Sometimes, violent incidents might still spill onto your campus even if you and your school resource officers are supporting your students to refrain from fighting. You can't control what happens off campus that can affect your students on campus. Having those relationships already built with students and school police will help you to collaborate with your school resource officers, hall monitors, and administration when there is a potential problem.

Collaborate with your school police to create a culture of prevention. School and student safety are vastly improved when teachers, school leaders, and police work together. You can't work with school police to stop issues before they happen if you don't already have a relationship with them.

4. *Step in when you see school police overstep their role.*

Just like teachers disproportionately discipline Black students, so do school police. When you witness it, intervene. Admittedly, this can be a scary thing to do. Make no mistake about that. Some school police officers are not collegial, and talking to them about some issues might be difficult. So use your professional judgment when deciding how to intervene.

If you see a school resource officer overstepping their role and trying to discipline a student for being tardy, swearing, or dress code infractions, and you have a relationship with them and feel safe intervening, step in and say, "Sir/Ma'am, I can take care of that." If you know a school resource officer tends to overstep their role, and they ask you if everything is okay when a student is acting out, tell them you got it. If you don't have everything under control, call your administrator for support.

When the teachers Black students need see their school police colleagues discipline or recommend consequences for students that violate school rules, they should insist that school police allow them to take responsibility for the student and their behavior concerns. Most officers will be happy to allow you to do this, as their primary responsibility is intervening when the law is broken. Again, use your professional judgment.

Teachers Must Know What School Police Misconduct Is and How to Address It

Police misconduct occurs when police officers violate people's civil rights while acting in their official capacity. False arrest, excessive use of force, searches without probable cause, seizing students' belongings without proper justification, and failing to investigate sexual harassment or assault complaints are all examples of police misconduct. When I was a school principal, teachers would tell me if they felt the school police overstepped their authority or used force excessively. Teachers told me when their students reported incidents to school police but felt the concerns they reported were disregarded. It happened rarely, but it did happen, and I was thankful "ranking officers" on my campuses intervened when students did not feel "heard" by law enforcement.

There are a few places you can turn to report police misconduct. You can go to the US Department of Education's Office of Civil Rights webpage and file a complaint. Most school districts have a process for filing complaints, so you can take that avenue. You can also report police misconduct to nonprofit organizations such as the ACLU, your local branch of the NAACP, or the Education Justice Alliance. You can file a complaint with your state department of education.

If the police in your school are officers from your local police force, you can file a complaint with their office. Document problematic incidents with school police officers. Note the time, date, location, and details about the problematic behavior. It is scary to report police misconduct, so you must decide how you would like to proceed. Often, you will be required to sign your statement of complaint. The process of reporting police misconduct varies from state to state.

3–2–1 Chapter Reflection

Take a moment to reflect on the content of the chapter and what it means to you.

What are three important ideas from this chapter?

_____
_____
_____

What are two action steps you can take based on this chapter?

_____
_____
_____

What is one concept you would like to explore in more depth?

_____
_____
_____

References

Bell Weixler, L., Jr., Harris, N., Gerry, A., & Tulane University. (2020). *Voices of new Orleans youth: What do the city's young people think about their schools and communities?* Survey Report. https://educationresearchalliancenola.org/files/publications/20200608-Weixler-et-al-Voices-of-New-Orleans-Youth-What-Do-the-Citys-Young-People-Think-About-Their-Schools-and-Communities.pdf

Ellis, N. T. (2022, June 9). *Experts worry about a heavier police presence in schools: 'Black and brown children bear the brunt of criminalization'.* CNN. www.cnn.com/2022/06/07/us/school-officers-impact-on-black-students/index.html

Graf, N. (2024, April 14). *A majority of U.S. teens fear a shooting could happen at their school, and most parents share their concern*. Pew Research Center. www.pewresearch.org/short-reads/2018/04/18/a-majority-of-u-s-teens-fear-a-shooting-could-happen-at-their-school-and-most-parents-share-their-concern/

Hurst, K. (2024, April 11). *About 1 in 4 U.S. Teachers say their school went into a gun-related lockdown in the last school year*. Pew Research Center. www.pewresearch.org/short-reads/2024/04/11/about-1-in-4-us-teachers-say-their-school-went-into-a-gun-related-lockdown-in-the-last-school-year/

Mitchell, C., Yerardi, J., & Ferriss, S. (2021, September 9). School policing falls hardest on Black students and those with disabilities, study shows. *USA Today*. www.usatoday.com/story/news/investigations/2021/09/08/police-schools-black-and-disabled-children-face-harsher-discipline/5436023001/

Nakamoto, J., Cerna, R., & Stern, A. (2017). *High school students' perceptions of police vary by student race and ethnicity*. Findings from an analysis of the California Healthy Kids Survey, 2017/18. www.wested.org/wp-content/uploads/2019/05/resource-high-school-students-perceptions-of-police.pdf

Police in schools: Developments, issues, and best practices. (2021). www.americanbar.org/content/dam/aba/publications/litigation_committees/childrights/policing-in-schools/policing-in-schools-memo.pdf

Police in schools have outsize effect on Black children, report says. (2022, December 29). *NBC News*. www.nbcnews.com/news/nbcblk/report-police-schools-outsize-effect-black-children-rcna63523

Safe and Sound Schools, Raptor Technologies, & Lightspeed Systems. (2022). *2022 State of school safety report* [Report]. https://safeandsoundschools.org/wp-content/uploads/2022/08/State-of-School-Safety-Report-FINAL.pdf

Sorensen, L., & Avila-Acosta, M. (2023, September 7). Navigating the tradeoffs of police in schools. *Brookings.* www.brookings.edu/articles/navigating-the-tradeoffs-of-police-in-schools/

U.S. Education Department's office for Civil Rights releases new civil rights data on students' access to educational opportunities during the pandemic. (n.d.). U.S. Department of Education. www.ed.gov/news/press-releases/us-education-departments-office-civil-rights-releases-new-civil-rights-data-students%E2%80%99-access-educational-opportunities-during-pandemic

Epilogue

Final Thoughts About Being a Teacher Black Students Need

This book focuses on improving the educational experience of Black children, as I am keenly concerned about how my children and other Black children experience school. The simple truth of the matter is that schooling should amplify the human "being" of all children, and the strategies in this book will help you do that.

It is urgently important that teachers meet all students' needs, including Black students. Black students have a right to an education that prepares them for the American dream of opportunity, upward mobility, freedom, equal justice under the law, and economic success for anyone willing to work hard to attain it.

Admittedly, there's an uphill climb to ensure that you meet the needs of your Black students. Not only do you have to teach state standards in ways your Black students can master like scaffolding instruction and teaching in culturally relevant ways – best practices that help all students – but you must also do so in ways that overcome barriers caused by resource inequality, racial bias and discrimination, socioeconomic strain, school segregation, and a lack of mental health services and supports.

Compounding these barriers are other things that you don't directly control, such as inequitable school funding, other teachers' implicit biases, and cultural mismatch that may exist between Black students, you and their other teachers, and the expectations of their schools. Regardless, you must ensure that your Black students are educated in ways that prepare them for success in life.

This book acts as a guide to help you navigate your uphill climb as you support your Black students and create the environment they need to thrive in your classroom and at your school. Lean on this book when you need support, and refer to it often. As a former teacher and school district leader, I know you have a lot on your plate. Adopt one new practice from this book at a time, and over time, they'll be naturally interwoven into your pedagogy.

While this book focuses on the needs of Black students, the strategies and recommendations are best practices, often backed by research, that benefit all students. As a busy teacher who took the time to read this book, I know you want to make sure that all of your students have a fantastic experience learning, growing, and maturing into fine young men and women.

The strategies in this book aim to create more inclusive, equitable, and supportive classrooms where teachers hold high expectations for all learners. These strategies will decrease the degree to which Black students feel marginalized in school communities and nurture classroom environments where all students feel a sense of belonging in their classrooms and schools. Every child deserves a free and appropriate public education, and the strategies in this book will help educators ensure schooling benefits all children.

Before I wrap up this book, I want to highlight the importance of your relationships with your Black students and the weight it carries in their lives. Black students will have many teachers throughout schooling. Be one of the teachers that uplifts them. Too many students already have teachers who, sometimes unconsciously, tear them down and crush their spirits.

It is a fact that adults' expectations of students in schools shape students' academic performance and behavior (Gentrup et al., 2020). When teachers under expect from students and over-discipline, it disempowers students and undermines their ability to be successful in class. The phenomenon of self-fulfilling prophecy is real. When teachers believe Black students can perform just as well as their non-Black peers, Black students overwhelmingly do better in school (Morrison, 2020). Believe that all of your students can and will be academically and behaviorally successful in your classes.

Focus on creating positive and relevant classroom experiences for your Black students that make your classroom a safe space where they want to be and that prepare them to accomplish their dreams and goals. As a teacher, you have a tremendous influence on how your students experience school (Raab, 2020). When Black students like their teacher, they are more engaged in schooling, have more positive feelings about their teacher's class, and tend to be high achievers (Royston, 2015). The logic seems so simple, but too often, Black students feel disconnected from their teachers and school, and when they do, too often, Black students who feel disconnected from their teachers and school get pushed out of school altogether or pushed away from great school experiences (Meyer, 2012).

Having genuine, positive relationships with [your] Black students [is vital]. Black students will do what you tell them to do, simply because they like you.

Those of you who read my book *Restorative Justice Tribunal* know that I was the principal at a school that was volatile, affected by gang violence, and where students shouldered unimaginable trauma in their home lives. To successfully teach at that school, staff HAD to form relationships with their students. Teachers who did not have positive relationships with their students rarely taught in that school for more than a year. It was through genuine, positive relationships that teachers kept students safe and away from harm as well as focused on teaching and learning.

Yes, it is important that your Black students like you. But let me be clear. You are the teacher, and your relationships with students must be defined by appropriate boundaries, professionalism, and a genuine concern for their personal and educational well-being. I've seen teachers use foul language in class, say inappropriate things, or do things that blur professional boundaries in attempts to appear "cool" to students. Please don't do that. Children want and need structure, and one of those structures is a clear behavioral boundaries around adults. Your relationship with students is built, in part, on those boundaries.

Your relationships with your students and how you teach them will live in their hearts and minds forever. That is a massive responsibility that I know you are able to meet. Thank you for your willingness to be curious, vulnerable, and caring throughout your journey as a teacher. Thank you for everything you do to be a teacher Black students need.

References

Gentrup, S., Lorenz, G., Kristen, C., & Kogan, I. (2020). Self-fulfilling prophecies in the classroom: Teacher expectations, teacher feedback and student achievement. *Learning and Instruction*, *66*, 101296. https://doi.org/10.1016/j.learninstruc.2019.101296

Meyer, P. (2012, August 20). *The discipline dilemma: Why Black kids draw the short straw on suspensions*. The Thomas B. Fordham Institute. https://fordhaminstitute.org/ohio/commentary/discipline-dilemma-why-black-kids-draw-short-straw-suspensions

Morrison, N. (2020, December 16). If you want Black students to do well at school, it helps if you're positive about Black students. *Forbes.* www.forbes.com/sites/nickmorrison/2020/12/16/if-you-want-black-students-to-do-well-at-school-it-helps-if-youre-positive-about-black-students/

Raab, E. L. (2020, April 29). Student experience, not outcomes, matter most for school design. *Medium.* https://medium.com/reenvisioned/practice-makes-perfect-6cd77d70b122

Royston, L. (2015, December 23). *Yes, it's important that your students like you.* Education & Teacher Conferences. www.learningandthebrain.com/blog/students-like-you/

Printed in the United States
by Baker & Taylor Publisher Services